3703123833

SHAPE ANALYSIS AND RETRIEVAL OF MULTIMEDIA OBJECTS

MULTIMEDIA SYSTEMS AND APPLICATIONS SERIES

Consulting Editor

Borko Furht
Florida Atlantic University

Recently Published Titles:

SHAPE ANALYSIS AND RETRIEVAL OF MULTIMEDIA OBJECTS

by

Maytham H. Safar
Kuwait University, Kuwait

Cyrus Shahabi
University of Southern California, U.S.A.

KLUWER ACADEMIC PUBLISHERS
Boston / Dordrecht / London

Distributors for North, Central and South America:
Kluwer Academic Publishers
101 Philip Drive
Assinippi Park
Norwell, Massachusetts 02061 USA
Telephone (781) 871-6600
Fax (781) 681-9045
E-Mail: kluwer@wkap.com

Distributors for all other countries:
Kluwer Academic Publishers Group
Post Office Box 322
3300 AH Dordrecht, THE NETHERLANDS
Telephone 31 78 6576 000
Fax 31 78 6576 254
E-Mail: services@wkap.nl

 Electronic Services < http://www.wkap.nl >

Library of Congress Cataloging-in-Publication Data

A C.I.P. Catalogue record for this book is available
from the Library of Congress.

Safar, Maytham H.; Shahabi, Cyrus
SHAPE ANALYSIS AND RETRIEVAL OF MULTIMEDIA OBJECTS
ISBN: 1-4020-7252-X

Printed on acid-free paper.

Printed in Great Britain by IBT Global, London

Contents

List of Figures

List of Tables

Preface

With the explosive growth of multimedia applications, the ability to index/retrieve multimedia objects in an efficient way is challenging to both researchers and practitioners. A major data type stored and managed by these applications is representation of two dimensional (2D) objects. Objects contain many features (e.g., color, texture, shape, etc.) that have meaningful semantics. From those features, shape is an important feature that conforms with the way human beings interpret and interact with the real world objects. The shape representation of objects can therefore be used for their indexing, retrieval, and as a similarity measure. The object databases can then be queried and searched for different purposes. For example, a CAD application for manufacturing industrial parts might intend to reduce the cost of building new industrial parts by searching for reusable existing parts in a database. For an alternative trade mark registry application, one might need to ensure that a new registered trademark is sufficiently distinctive from the existing marks by searching the database. Besides similarity matching, many other applications require to represent and process spatial relations between objects. Two important types of spatial queries are: topological and direction queries. With topological queries, we are interested in finding objects that are in the neighborhood, incident, or included in the query object. While, with direction queries, we are interested in finding the objects that satisfy a certain location in space (north, south) with respect to the query object.

Based on the above discussion we can identify an important basic problem: given a query object, a set of similar objects or objects satisfying some spatial relation should be retrieved without accessing all the objects in the database. Efficient solutions to this problem have important applications in database, image and multimedia information systems as well as other potential application domains. There are two obstacles for efficient execution of whole match queries. First, the general problem of comparing two 2D objects under rotation, scaling, and translation invariance is known to be computationally expensive. Second, the size of the multimedia and CAD databases are growing and hence given a query object the matching objects should be retrieved without accessing all the objects in the database.

In this book, we present a new shape-based object retrieval technique based on minimum bounding circles (MBCs). Our proposed MBC-based method can be used for efficient retrieval of 2D objects by utilizing three different index structures on features that are extracted from the objects' MBCs. Furthermore, we provide metrics and criterions to evaluate and compare the effectiveness and robustness of different shape retrieval methods. Besides similarity retrieval, we describe the support of spatial queries (e.g., topological and direction queries) using spatial data structures also based on MBC. This book provides a comprehensive survey of the most advanced and powerful shape retrieval techniques used in practice. In addition, it addresses key methodological issues for evaluation of shape retrieval methods. It is intended for undergraduate, graduate students, and researchers in the field of multimedia databases, information retrieval, image retrieval, shape analysis, data mining, geographic information systems, and digital libraries. The concepts and techniques can be used for the representation, indexing, and querying of visual shapes.

1.   Outline

Chapter 1 describes various methods for shape representation and in Chapter 2 we describe what is used as similarity comparison during the query processing process. Chapter 3 lists different image shape features that are used by the different shape representation techniques for organizing the useful shape information in index structures for efficient retrieval. Next we present a general background and provide an overview of definitions and notations used in this book. In Chapter 4 we briefly describe four boundary based methods for shape representation and retrieval. Chapters 5 and 6 describe how to support similarity queries and support spatial queries, respectively. Following that, Chapter 7 briefly describes multidimensional index structures that can be used to support shape retrieval queries. In addition, it explains in details three alternative index structures based on *MBC* features. In Chapter 8, we show how to expedite the processing of spatial queries by using the *Sphere-tree* index structure. Then, we address the mismatch between approximation relations and actual relations for intermediate nodes of the tree, and how to handle complex queries. Chapter 9 begins by addressing key methodological issues for the evaluation of shape retrieval methods with real data and under different scenarios [72, 73]. We describe several metrics and criterions to evaluate the effectiveness of a given shape representation technique based on : 1) accuracy in terms of recall and precision, 2) computation and storage costs, 3) sensitivity to noise and boundary points representing a shape, 4) support for different query types, and 5) impact of human perception. Finally, in Chapter 10 we explain two optimization techniques that further improve the performance of MBC-based shape retrieval method in several aspects.

Appendix 1 describes the algorithm used to find the minimum bounding circle of an object, and provides the cost analysis of the index structures. Appendix 2 describes the primitive topological and direction relation sets as defined in [25, 62, 63, 64, 92]. We start by defining the primitive topological relations as defined by the 9-intersection model for objects represented by their MBR. Then we define the two topological relation sets $mt1$ and $mt2$ as defined in [64]. Finally, Appendix 2 describes and compares the efficiency of the alternative shape representation techniques in terms of computation and storage requirements.

2. Acknowledgements

The work presented in this book could not have been possible without the guidance and support of many people. First, and foremost, I would like to acknowledge and thank the help of my co-editor, Dr. Cyrus Shahabi, who has provided me with substantial assistance. He gave me the opportunity of pursuing this work and directing my efforts to complete it. I wish to thank our editors at Kluwer academic publishers, Susan Lagerstrom-Fife and Sharon Palleschi for their confidence and patience in working with us on the project. Last, but not least, I would like to thank my parents for their encouragement, my wife for proofreading the book and my friends for their support, faith in my abilities to accomplish anything I set out to do, and for being a source of motivation and encouragement.

MAYTHAM SAFAR

For F.A.T. and F.A.B.
with best regards

Contributing Authors

Maytham Safar is currently an Assistant Professor at the Computer Engineering Department, Kuwait University. He received his B.S. degree in Computer Engineering from Kuwait University in 1992, his M.S. degree in Electrical Engineering from University of Colorado at Boulder in 1995, and Ph.D. degree in Computer Science from the University of Southern California in 2000. He has articles, book chapters, and conference papers in the areas of databases and multimedia. Dr. Safar's current research interests include image retrieval, shape representation, spatial index structures, spatial databases, multimedia databases, and data mining.

Cyrus Shahabi is currently an Assistant Professor and the Director of the Information Laboratory at the Computer Science Department of the University of Southern California (USC). He is also the Director of the Information Management Research Area at the Integrated Media Systems Center (IMSC), an NSF Engineering Research Center at USC. He received his M.S. and Ph.D. degrees in Computer Science from the University of Southern California in August 1993 and 1996, respectively. His B.S. degree is in Computer Engineering from Sharif University of Technology at Tehran. He has articles, book chapters, and conference papers in the areas of databases and multimedia. Dr. Shahabi's current research interests include multidimensional databases, multimedia servers, and data mining.

Introduction

Several applications in the areas of CAD/CAM and computer graphics require to store and access large databases. A major data type stored and managed by these applications is representation of two dimensional (2D) objects. Objects contain many features (e.g., color, texture, shape, etc.) that have meaningful semantics. From those features, shape is an important feature that conforms with the way human beings interpret and interact with the real world objects. The shape representation of objects can therefore be used for their indexing, retrieval, and as a similarity measure.

The object databases can be queried and searched for different purposes. For example, a CAD application [9] for manufacturing might intend to reduce the cost of building new industrial parts by searching for reusable existing parts in a database. For an alternative trade mark registry application [17], one might need to ensure that a new registered trademark is sufficiently distinctive from the existing marks by searching the database. Meanwhile, new multimedia applications such as structured video [30], animation, and *MPEG-7* standard [89] define specific objects that constitute different scenes of a continuous presentation. These scenes and their objects can be stored in a database for future queries. A sample query might be *"find all the scenes that contain a certain object"*. Therefore, one of the important functionalities required by all these applications is the capability to find objects in a database that match a given object.

There are two categories of match queries: *whole matching* and *partial matching* queries. With whole matching, a query object is compared with a set of objects to find the ones that are either exactly identical or similar to the query object. With partial matching, however, we are interested in finding the objects that have parts that match the query object. In this work, we concentrate on whole matching and do not discuss partial matching in detail. We focus on different variations of match queries (**EM**, **RST**, and **SIM**) to cover cases where the database is searched for exactly identical objects; identical objects that are rotation, scaling, and translation invariant (termed *I-RST*) or identical objects with a specified rotation angle (R), scaling factor (S), translation vector (T), or any combination of the three $(S\text{-}RST)$; or *similar* objects per our definition of similarity.

There are two obstacles for efficient execution of whole match queries. First, the general problem of comparing two 2D objects under rotation, scaling, and translation invariance is known to be computationally expensive [3]. Second, the size of the multimedia and CAD databases are growing and hence given a query object the matching objects should be retrieved without accessing all the objects in the database.

Besides similarity matching, many other applications in the areas of cartography, computer vision, spatial reasoning, cognitive science, image and multimedia databases, and geographic applications require to represent and process spatial relations between objects. Two important types of spatial queries are: *topological* and *direction* queries. With topological queries, we are interested in finding objects that are in the neighborhood, incident, or included in the query object. While, with direction queries, we are interested in finding the objects that satisfy a certain location in space (*e.g. north*, *south*) with respect to the query object. For the example of multimedia applications, here a sample query might be *"find all the scenes that an object (A) is on the top or near an object (B)"*. Therefore, one of the important functionalities required by all of these applications is the capability to find objects in a database that satisfies a spatial relation with a given object.

In a spatial database system, the objects are organized and accessed by spatial access methods $(SAMs)$. However, since $SAMs$ are not able to organize complex polygon objects directly, a common strategy is to store object approximations and use these approximations to index the data space. Approximations maintain the most important features of the objects (position and extension) and therefore they can be used to efficiently *estimate* the result of a spatial query. The advantage of using approximations is that the exact representation of the object is not often required to be loaded into main memory and be examined by expensive and complex computational geometry algorithms. Instead, relationships between the approximations of the objects (*MBC*s or *MBR*s) can be examined quite efficiently. Therefore, a typical technique to improve the performance of spatial queries, is to examine the objects' approximations instead of the actual representations of the objects (typically represented by *polygons*). The problem, however, is that by using objects' approximations we introduce *false hits* (in which the relation between the approximations is a superset of the relations between the actual objects). Thus, a successful approximation is the one that reduces the number of false hits.

Based on the discussions above we can identify an important basic problem: given a query object, a set of similar objects or objects satisfying some spatial relation should be retrieved without accessing all the objects in the database. Efficient solutions to this problem have important applications in database, image and multimedia information systems as well as other potential application domains.

The size of databases are growing, and comparing two 2D objects under rotation, scaling, and translation invariance is known to be computationally expensive. Hence it is very important to find a shape representation technique of objects that can be efficiently used for their indexing, retrieval, and as a similarity measure. The shape representation technique should be capable of extracting object features that: have good discriminating capabilities; are invariant to scale, translation and rotation; are simple to extract and require low storage and computational costs. In addition, the shape representation technique should be robust and stable under *"uncertainty"* issues and situations. Uncertainty can be a consequence of several factors, for example the assumptions that perfect data is always presented in the database, or that all shape representation methods represent the objects similarly are not valid.

The necessity of supporting spatial querying in many other applications also motivates identifying shape features that could be used efficiently to both represent the objects and support such queries. Since complex polygon objects are hard to organize directly using spatial access methods, approximations of the objects are usually used. Hence, it is important that the shape representation technique be able to approximate the objects and at the same time: maintain their most important features, reduce the complexity of the algorithms required to define relationships between the objects and reduce the number of false hits.

3.   Shape Representation

There are various methods for shape representation in the literature. Overviews of shape representation techniques are provided in [53, 91], which categorize techniques into different categories (e.g., *boundary* or *region* based categories). A drawback of these overviews is that they sometimes miscategorize some techniques. For example, they categorize spatial similarity based techniques (where the retrieval of objects is performed based on the spatial relationships among objects) as shape retrieval techniques. Another drawback is that they do not provide a clear criteria on which the categorization is based. Therefore, we introduce a new shape description taxonomy, in which we break the techniques into two categories: *boundary* and *region* based techniques. We further breakdown each category into *transformation* and *spatial* (measurement) sub-categories. Finally, the spatial sub-category is broken into *partial* and *complete* techniques depending on whether the techniques/features use partial parts of the shape or the whole shape. We also added further techniques that were not described in previous studies [53, 91] (e.g., turning angle, collinearity, ...etc.).

4.   Why MBC?

We compare four boundary based methods for shape representation and retrieval: *Fourier descriptors* method (FD) [31, 41, 75] (based on objects' shape radii), *grid*-based method (GB) [50, 77] (based on chain codes), *Delaunay triangulation* method (DT) [90, 91] (based on corner points) and MBC-based methods (based on minimum bounding circles and *angle sequences*). FD and GB are the more established methods that were used in some commercial systems [53] and as a basis for different comparison studies [53, 77], while DT is a new *histogram* -based approach of shape representation. MBC-based methods are our approach to shape representation and similarity measure. Although MBC-based methods use simple attributes such as minimum bounding circles and angle sequences (simple to extract), these attributes were shown to be *translation*, *rotation*, and *scale* invariant in [85]. In addition, the similarity retrieval accuracy of one of our MBC-based methods (MBC-$TPVAS$) is comparable to the other methods, while it has the lowest computation cost to generate the shape signatures of the objects. Moreover, it has low storage requirement, and a comparable computation cost to compute the similarity between two shape signatures. In addition, our

MBC-based method requires no normalization of the objects. Furthermore, the experiments demonstrate the robustness of MBC-$TPVAS$ under various scenarios of uncertainty compared to the other methods. The results show that MBC-$TPVAS$ is not very sensitive to noise and perturbations on the shape vertices and outperformed other methods. The results also show that MBC-$TPVAS$ is not very sensitive to the corner points detection algorithm (VRA) and observes less degradation in precision than the other methods. Finally, with the MBC-based method, a subset of the MBC features (*e.g., radius r, center C, and start point SP*) could be utilized to support S-RST query types. The other three methods $(FD, DT,$ and $GB)$ lack the support of S-RST queries. This is due to either the use of normalization, or lack of features that could support such queries.

5.   MBC for Similarity Queries

There are two obstacles for efficient execution of *match* queries. First, the general problem of comparing two 2D objects under *rotation, scaling*, and *translation* invariance is known to be computationally expensive. Second, the size of the multimedia and CAD databases are growing and hence given a query object the matching objects should be retrieved without accessing all the objects in the database. We address both obstacles collectively by identifying some features that can be extracted from the objects *Minimum Bounding circle* (MBC). These features can help us in both reducing the complexity of comparison algorithms and building index structures to search only a subset of the candidate objects for match queries.

We focus on three variations of match queries (**EM, RST**, and **SIM**) to cover cases where the database is searched for exactly identical objects; identical objects that are rotation, scaling, and translation invariant $(I$-$RST)$ or within a specified rotation angle, scaling factor, and a translation vector $(S$-$RST)$; or *similar* objects per our definition of similarity. In some application domains, the support of S-RST query types is important. An example is, searching for similar tumor shapes in a medical image database [46]. Tumors are presented by a set of 2D images that represent slices through it. A method for retrieving similar tumor shapes would help to discover correlations between tumor shape and certain diseases. Besides the shape, the size and the location of the tumor would help in the identification of patients with similar health history. To expedite the performance of all these variations, we identify a set of six features that could be extracted from the MBC of each object. Different subsets of object's MBC features are then used to build three alternative index structures I_{TPAS} , I_{VAS} , and I_{TPVAS} . Final storage and retrieval of the features are enhanced further by incorporating multidimensional index structures, (*e.g.* R*-tree). For designing our index structures we take into consideration the completeness of the model; *i.e.* it reduces the number of *false hits* and guarantees no *false drops*. In the final step, by utilizing our feature-based variations of comparison algorithms, we eliminate all the false hits. In [72, 71] we compared the performance of four different shape representation techniques (*i.e.*, *FD*, *GB*, *DT*, and *MBC-TPVAS*). The results demonstrated the effectiveness of our MBC-based index structures. First, our results show that some methods (e.g., *MBC-TPVAS*) have better accuracy than others in the presence of noise. Second, while some methods may have a comparable computation cost to compute the similarity between two shape signatures, however, some techniques (e.g., *MBC-TPVAS*) have much lower computation cost to generate the shape signatures of the objects. Third, some techniques (e.g., *MBC-TPVAS*) are less sensitive than others to the number of vertices used to represent a shape. Finally, the results show that some methods (i.e., *MBC-TPVAS*) have direct support for other query types (such as *S-RST* and spatial queries), while others lack to support them.

6. MBC for Spatial Queries

Almost all the previous studies on spatial databases use the *minimum bounding rectangle* (*MBR*) of an object as its approximation [12, 25, 33, 64, 66]. In this book, however, we focus on the *minimum bounding circle* (*MBC*s) of an object as its approximation. Our primary motivation for this decision is that, we have shown previously the interesting properties of MBC to improve the efficiency of similarity queries for the retrieval of 2D objects by shape. Therefore, in order to utilize the same approximation for other spatial queries (i.e., topological and direction queries) , we investigated the usefulness and feasibility of MBCs for such queries. We show how a subset of MBC features could also be utilized to answer spatial queries. As a result, there is no need to maintain two approximations (*i.e.*, MBR and MBC) per object for efficient support of different queries (*i.e.*, similarity and spatial).

In addition, we argue that depending on the application, using MBC approximations can be more beneficial as compared to using MBRs. First, circles are insensitive to orientation and hence an object's MBC is unique and invariant to translation and rotation. This property suits the requirements of the topological relations in which MBCs stay invariant under topological transformations such as translation, rotation and scaling [64]. Second, in [57] an indexing technique (*Sphere-tree*), was proposed for circles that could be used to efficiently support MBC based spatial queries (see Chapter 8 for further details). Third, in applications where queries of type: *"finding neighbors within a distance"* are frequently submitted, and the query regions are irregular, MBCs are more suited than MBRs. Finally, circles occupy less storage space as compared to rectangles.

Moreover, we show that MBC is a successful approximation for topological overlap queries (important for intersection joins). We show that the performance of overlap queries can be improved by distinguishing among 9 different types of overlap between the MBCs. Then, we determine the cases in which the relations between the actual objects can be determined efficiently from the relations between their corresponding MBCs. Furthermore, we distinguish between *half-filled* and *fully--filled* MBCs, which helps in identifying special cases for *overlap* and *equal* relations that reduces the number of false hits even further. For direction relations, by employing the concept of *cone-directions* [66], we introduce two methods to reduce the number of false hits. We achieve that by partitioning the MBCs into regions, and find the direction between objects based on the regions they cover.

I

IMAGE SHAPE DESCRIPTION AND RETRIEVAL

Chapter 1

IMAGE DESCRIPTION TECHNIQUES

Shape-Based Image Description Techniques

Introduction

In the past few years, several applications in the areas of Multimedia information systems, CAD/CAM and computer graphics require to store and access large volumes of multimedia data such as images. Images can be associated with both low-level semantics (color, texture, shape, and various spatial constraints), and high-level semantics (correspondence between image objects and real-world objects). *"In order to deal with these rich semantics of images, it is necessary to move from image-level to object-level interpretation."* [91]. Therefore, a major data type stored and managed by these applications is the representation of two dimensional (2D) objects. Objects contain many features (e.g., color, texture, shape, etc.) that have meaningful semantics. From those features, shape is an important feature that conforms with the way human beings interpret and interact with the real world objects. Shape recognition has two major parts: shape description (representation) and shape matching. Shape description is an important issue in object recognition and its objective is to measure geometric attributes of an object, that can be used for classifying, matching, and recognizing objects. There are various methods for shape representation. There are also numerous shape matching approaches that have been proposed based upon the shape representation methods. The study in [53], categorizes shape description techniques into two classes: information preserving (IP)and non-information preserving (NIP), depending on whether or not it is possible to reconstruct an approximation of the object from the shape descriptors. Our application type requires that the system maintains an approximation of an object and does not require the reconstruction of the original objects from their descriptors (as in compression applications). Therefore, this work concentrates on NIP methods. Overviews of shape description techniques are provided in [53, 71, 90, 91].

1.   Shape Representation Methods

A study in [53], categorizes shape description techniques into two classes: information preserving (IP) or unambiguous, and non information preserving (NIP) or ambiguous, depending on whether or not it is possible to reconstruct an approximation of the object from the shape descriptors. The IP methods (such as [45]) are mostly used in data compression applications, where there is a need to reconstruct the original image. Our application type requires that the system maintains an approximation of an object and does not require the reconstruction of the original objects from their descriptors. Therefore, this chapter concentrates on NIP methods. An overview of shape description techniques is also provided in [53], which categorizes NIP techniques into two types, boundary based and region based techniques. Boundary based methods use only the contour of the objects shape, while, the region based methods use the internal details (e.g., holes) in addition to the contour. The

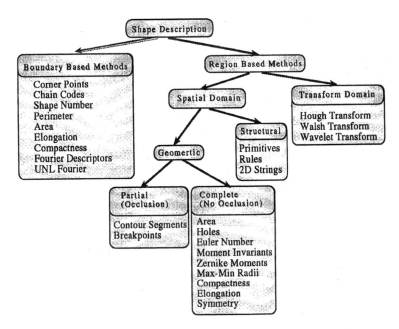

Figure 1.1.   Taxonomy of shape description techniques proposed by the study in [53]

region-based methods are further broken into spatial and transform domain sub-categories depending on whether direct measurements of the shape are used or a transformation is applied. The complete overview of this shape description technique is illustrated in Figure 1.1.

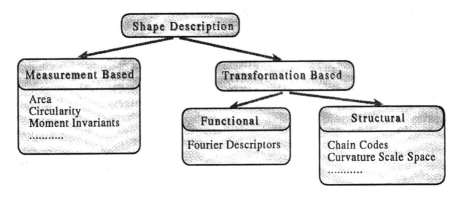

Figure 1.2. Taxonomy of shape description techniques proposed by the studies in [90, 91]

A drawback of this categorization is that it does not further sub-categorize boundary based methods into spatial domain and transform domain methods. For example, Fourier descriptors method can be considered as a transform domain technique, while chain codes can be considered as spatial domain technique. Another drawback of this categorization is that it assumes that structural techniques (e.g., 2D-strings) are a sub-category of region-based, spatial domain techniques. However, structural techniques as 2D-Strings can be considered as spatial similarity based techniques (where the retrieval of objects is performed based on the spatial relationships among objects) and not shape retrieval techniques (see Figure 1.3). In other studies [90, 91], shape description techniques are broken into two different categories: transformation-basedand measurement-based categories. Transformation-based category is further broken into two sub-categories: functional transformations (such as Fourier descriptors [67]) and structural transformations(such as chain codes [38]), however, it is not clear what criteria is used to this end. An overview of this shape description technique is illustrated in Figure 1.2. Some drawbacks of this categorization are that it does not distinguish between boundary or region based techniques, and sometimes it mis-categorizes some techniques. For example, chain code technique is categorized as a transformation-based technique, while it is a measurement-based technique. Another example is that silhouette moments could be used as a region-based technique but not as a boundary-based technique. To overcome the drawbacks of the previous shape description techniques, a new shape description taxonomy was introduced in [71], in which the techniques are broken into two sub-categories: boundary and region based techniques. They further breakdown each category into transformation and spatial (measurement) sub-categories. Finally, the spatial sub-category is broken into partial (occlusion) and complete (no occlusion) techniques depending on whether the techniques/features use partial parts of the shape or the whole shape. The complete taxonomy of this shape description technique is illustrated in Figure 1.3. This taxonomy added further techniques that were not described in [53, 90, 91] (e.g., turning angle, collinearity, etc.).

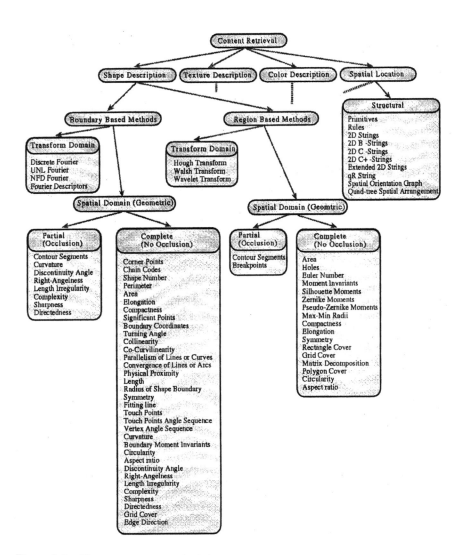

Figure 1.3. Taxonomy proposed of shape description techniques by the study in [71]

Chapter 2

IMAGE SIMILARITY MEASURES

Shape-based Image Similarity Measures

Introduction

The purpose of an image retrieval system is to organize and index images so that if we have a large number of images in the database, given a query image, the relevant images can be retrieved efficiently upon request. Relevant images is a list of images from the database which are most *"similar"* in some aspects to the query image. So the main issues of an image retrieval system are the proper indexing of images (see Chapter 7) and similarity comparison during the query process. In this chapter we consider the shape aspect of objects. Given a unique shape signature (based on boundary) for each object, the question is how to measure the distance and similarity between boundaries. For solving this problem, we need two things. First, a feature which represents the shape information of the image (see Chapter 3). Second, a similarity measure to compute the similarity between features of two images. The similarity measure is a matching function, and gives the degree of match or similarity for a given pair of images (represented by shape measures).

1. Similarity Measures

The similarity measure is expected to conform to human perception quite well. This is because human beings normally compare boundaries. When we want to compare two boundaries to see how much they differ, we prefer these two boundaries to be of the same or similar size. Then we rotate the boundaries to an orientation suitable for comparison. Finally, we overlay one boundary on top of the other to find how much they differ. Therefore, a desirable property of a similarity measure is that it should be a metric (that is, it has the properties of symmetry, transitivity and linearity). In addition, the similarity measure should be defined such that the larger the distance, the smaller the similarity. The advantage of this similarity measurement is that similar shapes will have high similarity resulting in high precision. In general for the purpose of matching and similarity computation, an image I can be represented by a feature vector f which captures different aspects of image content such as color information, texture features, shape information of objects in the image, spatial layout of the objects or any other content which may be of interest for the purpose of querying. Thus the image I can be represented as :

$$f = (i_1, i_2, \ldots, i_n) \tag{2.1}$$

where n is the number of content features. Once the image information is captured by the defined feature vector, the important thing to be determined is the similarity between any two images. The similarity between two images is computed using the feature vectors for any type of content-based similarity retrieval. The similarity measure is clearly application-dependent. Several similarity measures have been proposed in the literature for $1D$ and $2D$ signals that can also be applied for feature vectors. One of the typical similarity measures that is widely used as a comparison function is the *Euclidean distance*, also known as the standard n-dimensional L_2 metric. If we assume that the feature space is uniform, then the similarity measure between a pair of images Q and I having feature vector f^Q and f^I can be computed as the Euclidean distance between the two feature vectors. The uniformity assumption of the feature space implies that perceptual distances between points in the space correspond to the Euclidean metric. The similarity measure is therefore:

$$Dist(Q, I) = (\sum_{i=1}^{n}(f_i^Q - f_i^I)^2)^{\frac{1}{2}} \tag{2.2}$$

The distance between two identical images is zero, i.e $Dist(Q, Q) = 0$. Smaller values of distance $Dist()$ indicate more similarity between images and vice-versa. For similarity retrieval of images, the Euclidean distance $Dist(Q, I)$, can be computed between the query image and all the database images. The list can then be sorted based on the value of the distance in an increasing order. The output of such a retrieval is known as the ranked similarity output. Another similarity measure is the *weighted cross distance* function [55]. This metric takes the perceptual similarity between the different components (elements) of the feature vectors into account.

$$Dist(Q, I) = \sum_{i=1}^{n} \sum_{j=1}^{n} (1 - \frac{a_{ij}}{a_{max}})(f_i^Q - f_j^I)^2 \qquad (2.3)$$

where a_{ij} is the difference between f_i^Q and f_j^I, and a_{max} is the maximum difference between f_i^Q and f_j^I. A third weighted distance measure is derived from the standard n-dimensional L_1 metric, by taking into account the relative proportion of each feature vectors components [99].

$$Dist(Q, I) = \sum_{i=1}^{n} w_i((f_i^Q - f_i^I)^2)^{\frac{1}{2}} \qquad (2.4)$$

where w_i is f_i^Q if $f_i^Q > 0$ and $f_i^I > 0$; and is 1 if $f_i^Q = 0$ or $f_i^I > 0$. Most studies have chosen the Euclidean distance, because it can be used with any other type of similarity measure, as long as this measure can be expressed as the Euclidean distance between feature vectors in some feature space. In fact, the Euclidean distance is the optimal distance measure for estimation, if feature vectors are corrupted by noise (e.g., *Gaussian*). Thus if Q is our query and Q' is a corrupted version of it in the database, a searching method using the Euclidean distance should produce good results. Another valuable feature of the Euclidean distance is that it is preserved under orthonormal transforms. Other distance functions, like the L_p norms

$$L_p(Q, I) = (\sum_{i=1}^{n} |f_i^Q - f_i^I|^p)^{\frac{1}{p}} \qquad (2.5)$$

do not have this property, unless $p = 2$ ($L_2 \cong$ Euclidean distance).

Chapter 3

IMAGE SHAPE FEATURES

Boundary Based Shape Features

Introduction

Shape description or representation is an important issue in image analysis for object recognition and classification. The descriptions are given in terms of properties of objects contained in images and in terms of relationships between such objects. These properties correspond to characteristics of objects' position, size and shape. Each shape or image to be stored in the database is processed to obtain the shape features. Shape features are then used by the different shape representation techniques (see Chapters 4 and 7) for organizing the useful shape information in index structures for efficient retrieval. For example, boundaries (connected edges) capture the characteristics of the shape object. Therefore, shapes can be processed to obtain their shape boundaries. Then, the shape boundaries are automatically decomposed into a set of boundary points (interest points) that are commonly used in machine vision techniques for shape matching. The set of shape features is by no means unique. A given set of features can give acceptable results in retrievals for a specific set of applications. However, they may fail to give acceptable results for other set of applications. Therefore, any shape representation technique should extract the shape features that experts may deem appropriate for the application domain. Two types of features (i.e., *global* and *local*) are commonly used to describe objects [29]. *Global* features are the properties of objects that depend on their entire shape (e.g., area, perimeter). Since the entire shape is required to compute these properties, shape matching and retrieval techniques using global feature-based shape representation cannot handle images containing partially visible, overlapping, or touching objects. *Local* features are the structural features that can be computed from a shape's local regions. Examples are boundary segments and points of *maximal curvature* change. Techniques using local feature-based representations can handle images containing partially visible, overlapping, or touching objects. Shape features are used as shape similarity measures for shape-based retrieval in image databases. Therefore, they should be in accord with our visual perception and should meet the following criteria:

- **Should possess good discriminating capabilities.** Since complex polygon objects are hard to organize directly using spatial access methods, approximations of the objects are usually used. Hence, it is important that the shape representation technique be able to approximate the objects and at the same time maintain their most important features.

- **Invariant to affine transformations (i.e. rotations, scaling, and translation) of images.** This means that the shape feature of an object must not change when the original object is submitted to a certain set of affine geometric transformations, or an arbitrary combination of them. This is because, human beings ignore such variations in images for recognition and retrieval purposes. Hence, the features should not depend on scale, orientation, and position of objects.

- **Robust and abstract from distortion.** Since contours of objects in digital images are distorted due to digitization noise and due to segmentation errors, it is desirable to reduce the influence of noise and to neglect the distortions while at the same time preserving the perceptual appearances at the level sufficient for object recognition.

- **It should permit recognition of perceptually similar objects that are not mathematically identical.** *"Where a mathematical criterion would place a sharp dividing line, humans may have a fuzzy transition. Two shapes close to, but on opposite sides of this dividing line may appear quite similar to a human eye, even though their optimal descriptions are completely different"* [42].

- **Compact and easy to derive.** The size of databases are growing, and comparing two 2D objects under rotation, scaling, and translation invariance is known to be computationally expensive.

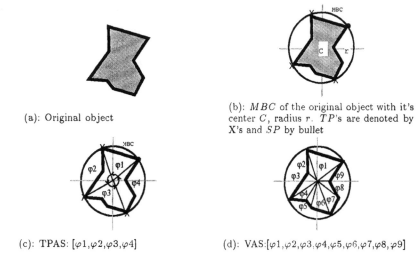

(a): Original object

(b): *MBC* of the original object with it's center *C*, radius *r*. *TP*'s are denoted by X's and *SP* by bullet

(c): TPAS: $[\varphi 1, \varphi 2, \varphi 3, \varphi 4]$

(d): VAS:$[\varphi 1, \varphi 2, \varphi 3, \varphi 4, \varphi 5, \varphi 6, \varphi 7, \varphi 8, \varphi 9]$

Figure 3.1. MBC features

Therefore, the shape features should be compact and easy to derive, and the calculation of similarity measure should be efficient.

- **A shape similarity measure should be universal.** For example, if we want to apply a shape similarity measure to distributed image databases (e.g., in Internet), where the object classes are generally unknown beforehand, it is necessary that the shape similarity measure be able to identify or distinguish objects of arbitrary shapes.

- **The representation scheme should be insensitive to scene complexity (occlusion, touching objects, etc.).** Hence shape matching and retrieval techniques should handle images containing partially visible, overlapping, or touching objects.

- **Similar shapes should have similar measures.** The similarity measure between shape representation should conform to human properties, i.e., perceptually similar shapes should have high similarity measures.

1.   MBC Features

We first describe a set of six features that could be extracted from the objects *MBC*s. These features are very important in our work since

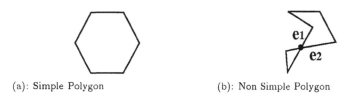

(a): Simple Polygon   (b): Non Simple Polygon

Figure 3.2.   Polygons

we will be using them for both indexing the objects and expediting the comparison between two objects. The six MBC features can be identified for each *simple polygon* object. A simple polygon is a polygon that has no pair of non-consecutive edges sharing a point (see Figure 3.2). In the rest of this paper we refer to *simple polygon* as polygon. The six MBC features are:

1 r: the radius of MBC

2 C: the coordinates of the center of MBC

3 TP: the set of touch points on MBC

4 $TPAS$: touch points angle sequence

5 VAS: vertex angle sequence

6 SP: the start point of the angle sequence

Figure 3.1 provides an example of an object with its six identified features. For the algorithms to extract the MBC features see Appendix 1.

Definition 1.1: *Minimum Bounding Circle*–**MBC** of an object is the closed disk of smallest radius containing all the points in the object (see Figure 3.1(b)). ∎

We denote MBC^i as the minimum bounding circle enclosing the object O^i. Each MBC^i is identified by its radius r^i and its center C^i.

Definition 1.2: *Touch Points*–**TP** of an object is the ordered set of points of the object that lays on the object's MBC (see Figure 3.1(b)). ∎

Definition 1.3: *Angle Sequence*–**AS** of an object is the sequence of angles contained between vectors connecting the center of the object's MBC and a subset of its points. ∎

Definition 1.4: *Start Point*–**SP** of an angle sequence is the point in the angle sequence that makes the smallest angle, counterclockwise; with the x-axis passing the center of the object's MBC (see Figure 3.1(b)). ∎

The angle sequence of the touch points (**TPAS**) of object O^i is $TPAS^i = [\theta_t^i]$; for $t = 0 \ldots n_{TP}^i - 1$. **TPAS** is a cyclic sequence of n_{TP}^i real numbers representing angles, where θ_j^i is the angle between two vectors (see Figure 3.1(c)). The angle sequence of all the vertices (**VAS**) of object O^i is $VAS^i = [\theta_t^i]$; for $t = 0 \ldots m^i - 1$; a cyclic sequence of m^i real numbers representing angles (see Figure 3.1(d)).

Given an object with m vertices, we could have m different ASs. Each representation depends on which vertex of the object is used as the start vertex from which the AS is computed. To reduce the number of possible AS representations of an object, we create the ASs of the objects by choosing the SPs as the start vertex. Since SP is a vertex in the set of touch points of an object, then in the worst case we might have the number of different AS representations equal to n_{TP}. For VAS we do not use the TP information, hence the number of starting points equals the number of vertices of the object.

We now define some extra features that could also be extracted from MBC and used later to reduce the number of false hits in the filter step. Hence, reducing the refinement step processing time by reducing the number of invocations of complex geometric algorithms.

Definition 1.5: *Separator-Diameter* of a circle is the diameter that separates the circle into two halves, one is empty and the other half containing the object (see Figure 6.4(a)). ∎

Definition 1.6: *Half-filled circle* is a circle that has a *separator-diameter* (see Figure 6.4(a)). ∎

Definition 1.7: *Fully-filled circle* is a circle in which any drawn diameter separates it into two halves, each half containing a part of the contained object (see Figure 6.4(b)). ∎

Lemma 1.8: *If a circle is half-filled, then at least two vertices of the actual object lay on the end points of the separator-diameter (see Figure 6.4(c)).*

Proof: The proof is by contradiction. Assume that we have an object q such that its MBC (MBC_q with diameter D_q) is *half-filled*, but has one vertex on the *separator-diameter*. In general, the largest Euclidean distance (D_{max}) between the vertices of an object (p) and any point in its MBC (MBC_p) should be *equal* to the diameter of MBC_p. In a *half-filled* circle, the equality occurs if and only if at least one vertex of the object is on an end point of the *separator-line* (diameter). Since we assumed that we have only one vertex of q on the *separator-line*, then the Euclidean distance between any vertex of q and a point in the half circle (except for the points on the *separator-line*) is $< D_q$ (*i.e.*, $D_{max} < D_q$). Consequently, we could find another circle with a diameter D_{new}, such that $D_{new} < D_q$ and includes all the vertices of q. This contradicts our assumption that the first circle was the MBC of the object. Therefore, for D_{max} to be *equal* to MBC_p, we must have two vertices of q to be at the end points of the *separator-diameter* (which also contradicts our assumption). ∎

We refer to the MBC of object q as $q\prime$, and use $RELATION(p,q)$ to define that p is related to q according to the relation $RELATION$. The query object/MBC is referred to as the *primary* object/MBC ($p/p\prime$). The object in the database to which the *primary* object/MBC is compared , is referred to as the *reference* object/MBC ($q/q\prime$). In the examples hereafter, the *reference* object, q, is the grey object, while the *primary* object p is the transparent object.

Chapter 4

ALTERNATIVE IMAGE DESCRIPTION TECHNIQUES

Shape-Based Image Description Techniques

Introduction

There is a variety of techniques that have been proposed in multimedia information systems area for shape representation [31, 41, 53]. Examples of those techniques are Fourier descriptors method (FD) [31, 41, 75] (based on objects' shape radii) and grid-based method (GB) [50, 77] (based on chain codes). They were used in some commercial systems [53] and as a basis for different comparison studies in [50, 53, 77, 78]. In addition, a new method based on a new indexing technique (i.e., Delaunay triangulation–DT) was proposed in [90]. With Delaunay triangulation, the shape features used are invariant under uniform translation, scaling, and rotation. However, with Delaunay triangulation, histogram-based representation is not very discriminative and is not unique, i.e., objects of different shapes may have the same feature point histogram representation. Also, choosing a histogram with a small number of bins provides less discriminating ability. Both Fourier descriptors and grid-based methods are variant to translation, rotation, and scaling. Therefore, shape signatures obtained for the same object with a different orientation in space or with a different scale will be different. Hence, given the shape signature of an object, a normalization procedure is required to normalize the object such that its boundary has a standard size and orientation. All in all, the GB, FD, and DT methods are unable to support S-RST query type. With the GB and FD methods, normalization is used so that the objects fit into a prespecified mesh, or the boundaries are forcied to have a standard size and orientation, respectively. While DT method representation provides no information about the size, and orientation of the original objects.

This chapter describes in brief four boundary based methods for shape representation and retrieval: Fourier descriptors method (FD) [31, 41, 75], grid-based method (GB) [50, 77], Delaunay triangulation method (DT) [90, 91], and our proposed $MBC\text{-}TPVAS$ method [84, 85].

1.   Fourier Descriptors Method

The FD method [32, 41, 50, 53, 75, 77, 78] obtains the object representation in the frequency domain as complex coefficients of the Fourier series expansion of the objects' shape signature. The method starts by obtaining a feature function of the object called shape signature $f(k)$; which could be curvature based, radius based, or boundary coordinates based. $f(k)$ is also called the Fourier descriptors (FDs) of the boundary. In the next step, a discrete Fourier transform of the shape signature is obtained. The Fourier coefficients obtained are then used for shape representation, as index, and for shape similarity calculation. The discrete Fourier transformation (DFT) of a shape signature $f(k)$ is given by:

$$F(u) = \frac{1}{N} \sum_{k=0}^{N-1} f(k) \exp(-j2\pi uk/N) \quad u = 0, 1, \dots, N-1 \qquad (4.1)$$

where N is the number of samples of $f(k)$.

Direct representation (e.g., radii) captures each individual details of a shape, however, it is very sensitive to small changes and noise. As a consequence, a small change in the coordinates of the objects' boundary points may lead to a very different shape signature, hence, very poor retrieval performance. On the other hand, Fourier transformation captures the general feature of a shape by converting the sensitive direct representation measures into frequency domain. As a result, the data is more robust to small changes and noise. Therefore, Fourier transformation is used as shape representation instead of the direct representation (see [50] for further details). The FDs are variant to rotation, and scaling. Therefore, given the FD of an object, a normalization procedure is required to normalize the object such that its boundary has a standard size, and orientation. In addition, the FD normalization should preserve all of the shape information. A popular shape signature is the shape radii (or centroidal distance) which computes the distance between points uniformly sampled along the object boundary and its centroid (its center of mass). When shape radii are used, only the dis-

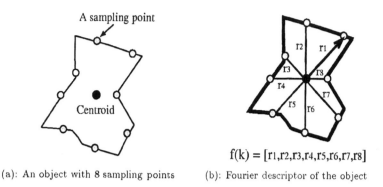

(a): An object with 8 sampling points   (b): Fourier descriptor of the object

Figure 4.1. Fourier descriptors method

tances between points are recorded and not the exact coordinates of the points. Thus, the shape signatures of the objects are translation invariant. Since the magnitude information of $F(u)$ (i.e., $|F(u)|$) is invariant to rotation, rotation normalization is achieved taking only the magnitude information from $F(u)$ and ignoring its phase information. Moreover, $|F(0)|$ reflects the energy of the shape radii, thus $|F(u)|/|F(0)|$ will be scale invariant. Therefore, in order to scale normalize the objects' FDs, the magnitude of all $F(u)$s are divided by the magnitude of $F(0)$. As a result of normalization a new feature vector, which is invariant to translation, rotation and scale, can be generated as follows: $FN = [|F(1)|/|F(0)||F(2)|/|F(0)|\dots|F(N)|/|F(0)|]^T$ [50].

The difference between two objects is defined as the Euclidean distance between their corresponding feature vectors. Hence, the similarity measure of FD method is that two objects are similar in shape, if and only if the Euclidean distance between their feature vectors is less than a prespecified threshold. In other words, they have the same set of distances between their centroids and their sampled boundary points.

An example is illustrated in Figure 4.1, where Figure 4.1(a) shows an object with its 8 sampling points and its centroid, and Figure 4.1(b) shows the radii distances and the Fourier descriptors $f(k)$ of the boundary.

2.   Grid Based Method

An alternative approach for shape representation is GB method [50, 53, 76, 77, 78] With this method, an object is first normalized for rotation and scale. Then, the object is mapped on a grid of fixed cell size. Subsequently, the grid is scanned and a 1 or 0 is assigned to the cells depending on whether the number of pixels in the cell which are inside the object are greater than or less than a predetermined threshold. Finally, a unique binary number is obtained as the shape representation by reading the 1's and 0's assigned to the cells from left to right and top to bottom. To improve the efficiency of this method, another shape feature, called *eccentricity* [77], was used. Eccentricity of shape is the ratio of the number of cells used in x-direction to the number of cells used in the y-direction to represent a shape. Therefore, for two objects to be similar, their shape signatures and their eccentricity values should be similar.

The difference between two objects is the number of cells in the grids which are covered by one shape and not the other, which is the same as the sum of 1's in the result of the exclusive OR of their binary numbers. Hence, the similarity measure of GB method is that two objects are similar in shape, if and only if the difference between their binary representations is less than a prespecified threshold, and they have similar eccentricities.

An example is illustrated in Figure 4.2, where the objects are mapped on to a grid of fixed cell size in a manner such that the objects are justified to the top left corner (i.e., assuming that the objects do not need to be normalized). The binary numbers obtained for the objects in Figure 4.2(a) and (b) are "110001110 111111111 111111111 111111110 111111100 001110000" and "000000110 000011100 001111100 111111100 111111110 011111111" respectively. Hence, the difference between the objects is 20.

A binary number obtained for the same object with a different orientation in space or with a different scale will be different. Therefore, the normalization of the object boundaries prior to indexing is crucial to meet the uniqueness criteria of the binary number.

2.1   Rotation Normalization

Rotation changes the spatial relationships between the grid cells and the objects' boundaries, which leads to different binary number representations for the same object. Therefore objects must be normalized for rotation. This is achieved by obtaining the *major axis* of the shape, which is the line joining the two points on the shape boundary farthest

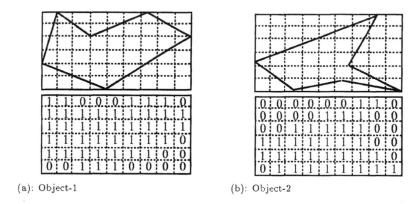

(a): Object-1   (b): Object-2

Figure 4.2.   Grid based method – object mapping and representation

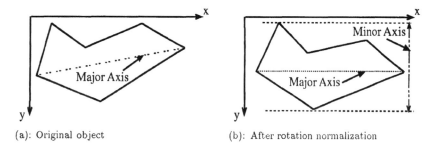

(a): Original object   (b): After rotation normalization

Figure 4.3.   Grid based method – rotation normalization

away from each other. Subsequently, the shape is rotated to make the major axis parallel to the x-axis. An example of rotation normalization of an object is shown in Figure 4.3, where in Figure 4.3(a) an object is shown prior to rotation normalization and Figure 4.3(b) shows the same object after being rotated so that the major axis becomes parallel to the x-axis.

2.2   Scale Normalization

Both the grid and the object sizes affect the binary number derived for an object. Therefore objects must be normalized for scale. This is achieved by choosing a fixed length of the major axis, called the *standardized major axis*. Subsequently, scaling normalization is achieved by scaling along the major axis of the object such that its major axis be-

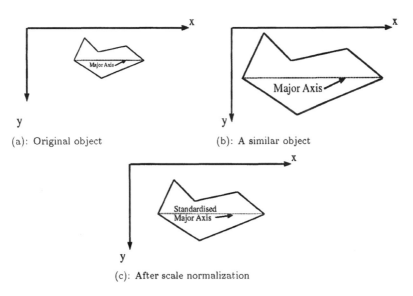

(a): Original object   (b): A similar object

(c): After scale normalization

Figure 4.4.   Grid based method – scale normalization

comes equal to the length of the standardized major axis. To maintain the perceptual similarity of the object, it is also scaled along the *minor axis* proportionally. The minor axis is perpendicular to the major axis and of such length that a rectangle with sides of major axis and minor axis defines the minimum bounding rectangle of the object. An example of scale normalization of an object is shown in Figure 4.4, where in Figure 4.4(a) and (b) two similar objects are shown prior to scale normalization while Figure 4.4(c) shows the same objects after being scaled along the x-axis and y-axis such that the length of the major axis becomes equal to the standardized major axis.

3.   Delaunay Triangulation Method

This approach of shape representation is *histogram-based* [90, 91]. Given an object, *corner points* are used as the feature points of the object. Corner points are generally *high-curvature* points located along the crossings of an object's edges or boundaries. Then a Delaunay triangulation of these feature points is constructed. Consequently, a feature point histogram is obtained by discretization of the angles produced by this triangulation into a set of bins and counting the number of times each discrete angle occurs in the triangulation. In building the feature point histogram, a selection criterion of which angles will contribute to the final feature point histogram is chosen. For example, the selection criterion could be counting the two largest angles, the two smallest angles, or all three angles of each individual Delaunay triangle.

The difference between two objects is the Euclidean distance between the corresponding bins of the objects' feature point histograms. Hence, the similarity measure of DT method is that two objects are similar in shape, if and only if the Euclidean distance between their feature point histograms is less than a prespecified threshold. In other words, they have the same set of feature points. Thus, each pair of the corresponding Delaunay triangles in the two resulting Delaunay triangulations must be similar to each other. The angles of the resulting Delaunay triangles of a set of points is invariant under uniform translations, scaling, and rotations. Therefore, the similarity measure is independent of object's position, scale, and rotation (i.e. objects do not have to be normalized). This approach also supports an incremental approach to image object matching, from coarse to fine, by varying the bin sizes.

An example is illustrated in Figure 4.5, where Figure 4.5(a) shows an object that consists of 10 feature points (corner points). Figure 4.5(b) shows the resulting Delaunay triangulation. While Figure 4.5 shows the resulting feature point histogram built by counting all three angles of each individual Delaunay triangle with bin size of 10 degrees.

4.   MBC-TPVAS Method

This approach, $TPVAS$, for shape representation was proposed by us in [84]. A major observation is that MBC features are unique per object. In addition, a subset of the MBC features (*e.g., TPAS, VAS, and TPs*) are translation, scaling and rotation independent. This subset of features could be utilized to support **SIM** and **RST** query types. We use object's SP to check if it is rotated, use object's r to check if it is scaled, and the vertex coordinates of the object's C to check if it is translated.

With $TPVAS$ method, the shape descriptor of an object depends on a subset of the six MBC features. The method starts by obtaining a feature function of the object called shape signature $f(k)$. To obtain $f(k)$, four steps are required. The minimum bounding circles of the objects are first found. Second, MBC features such as angle sequences (VAS) and number of touch points (TP) are identified. Third, the ob-

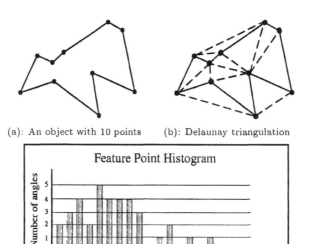

(a): An object with 10 points   (b): Delaunay triangulation

(c): Feature point histogram

Figure 4.5.   Delaunay triangulation method

jects' shape signature is identified as the sequence combination of TP and VAS. Finally, as with the FD method, a unique object representation is obtained as the discrete Fourier series expansion of the objects' shape signature. The Fourier coefficients obtained are used for shape representation, as index, and for shape similarity calculation. The discrete Fourier transformation (DFT) of a shape signature $f(k)$ is given by:

$$F(u) = \frac{1}{\sqrt{N}} \sum_{k=0}^{N-1} f(k) \exp(-j2\pi uk/N) \quad u = 0, 1, \ldots, N-1 \quad (4.2)$$

where N is the number of points in the polygon representation of an object.

Although $TPVAS$ method uses simple attributes such as minimum bounding circles and angle sequences, these attributes were shown to be translation, rotation, and scale invariant in [84]. Therefore, the similarity measure is independent of object's position, scale, and rotation (i.e. objects does not have to be normalized).

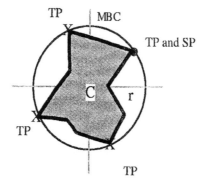

(a): An object with its MBC, center C, radius r, TP's, and SP

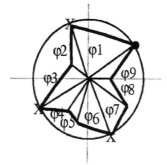

VAS $= [\varphi1,\varphi2,\varphi3,\varphi4,\varphi5,\varphi6,\varphi7,\varphi8,\varphi9]$
f(k) $= [TP,\varphi1,\varphi2,\varphi3,\varphi4,\varphi5,\varphi6,\varphi7,\varphi8,\varphi9]$

(b): Vertex angle sequence VAS and shape descriptor $f(k)$

Figure 4.6. MBC-TPVAS method

The difference between two objects is the Euclidean distance between their corresponding feature vectors. Hence, the similarity measure of $TPVAS$ is that two objects are similar in shape, if and only if the Euclidean distance between their feature vectors is less than a prespecified threshold. In other words, they have similar vertex angle sequences and number of touch points.

An example is illustrated in Figure 4.6. Figure 4.6(a) shows an object with 9 vertices with its minimum bounding circle, and touch points. Figure 4.6(b) shows the vertex angle sequence of the object and its shape descriptors $f(k)$.

II

QUERIES AND INDEX STRUCTURES IN THE WORLD OF MINIMUM BOUNDING CIRCLES

Chapter 5

SHAPE SIMILARITY MATCHING QUERIES

2D Similarity Queries in the World of Minimum Bounding Circles

Introduction

There are two categories of match queries: *whole matching* and *partial matching* queries. With whole matching, a query object is compared with a set of objects to find the ones that are either exactly identical or similar to the query object. With partial matching, however, we are interested in finding the objects that have parts that match the query object. In this chapter, we concentrate on whole matching and do not discuss partial matching in detail. We focus on three variations of match queries (**EM**, **RST**, and **SIM**) to cover cases where the database is searched for exactly identical objects; identical objects that are rotation, scaling, and translation invariant (termed *I-RST*) or identical objects with a specified rotation angle (R), scaling factor (S), translation vector (T), or any combination of the three $(S\text{-}RST)$; or *similar* objects per our definition of similarity. Various studies were conducted in the database area that address shape similarity matching queries. A group of the studies investigate techniques to speed up the similarity between 2-D objects based on shape [28, 29, 31, 41, 42, 53]. They investigated techniques to speed up the search of 2-D *"similar"* objects to a target object based on their shapes. This is somewhat similar to our **SIM** query type. For retrieving similar 2D polygon shapes from a CAD database system, previous work is presented in [28, 29, 42]. In [42] two 2-D polygons are considered similar if they have similar proportions of area. It assumes that polygon objects are constructed by the union of rectangles of different sizes. The major problem of their algorithm is that the representation is not unique and very sensitive to small changes in the coordinates of the rectangles. Also, the algorithm is not invariant against rotations, and it is limited to representing only polygon objects with sides parallel to the coordinate system. Therefore it can not guarantee no false drops. Some other works [28, 29], collect features from objects as a collection of a few adjacent interest points. Each object has more than one entry in the index. The major drawback of this approach is the use of nonlinear optimization, which is complex and time consuming, to calculate some parameters.

1.   2D Similarity Queries

In image information systems, our problem is as follows: assume that we have a large number of images in the database. Given a query image, we would like to retrieve or select all images that match or are visually *"similar"* in some aspect (here we consider the shape aspect) to the query image. This type of retrieval is called shape similarity based retrieval.

In general, a shape similarity based retrieval method should handle five major retrieval queries:

- **Retrieval of matching shapes (Full Match)**-Given a query shape, retrieve shapes that exactly match the given shape.

- **Retrieval of similar shapes (Approximate Match)**-Given a query shape, retrieve shapes that are similar (within some threshold of the similarity measure) to the query shape.

- **Retrieval of matching shapes with a specified transformation (Match with Specified Transformation)**Given a query shape, retrieve shapes that match the given shape with a specified rotation angle, scaling factor, translation vector , or any combination of the three.

- **Retrieval of matching shapes with unspecified transformation (Match with Unspecified Transformation)**-Given a query shape, retrieve shapes that match the given shape but are rotation, scaling, and translation invariant.

- **Retrieval of matching shapes with a specified combination of shape features (Partial Match)**-Given a query shape, retrieve shapes that match some features of a given shape.

1.1 Full Match

With this type of shape retrieval we are interested in answering the query *"find all shapes in a set of shapes that are exactly identical to the query shape"*. A full match for a given query shape is a database shape that has the correct shape in the correct position (i.e., they have the same shape, orientation, size, and the exact same dimensions). Full match searches are likely to be of little practical use for computer vision applications due to the noise and distortion inherent in image processing. However, they may be useful in computer graphics, CAD/CAM, multimedia, and computer cartography applications. Full match would be used, for example, if there is a large set of images, one of which has been reproduced and we now have to determine which. It is also *"the sort of thing humans do very well when riffling through the pages of a magazine for a particular page that we remember"* [42]. Full matches are point searches in the multidimensional index structure, precisely the kind of search where most point access methods (PAM)s (e.g. R-tree [39]) are designed to be most efficient. Having built an index structure, to perform a full match, the query shape is transformed in the same way as each data shape has been. We thus obtain a query point, and this point can be used as a key in an index search. Then, the query is processed by searching the index structure to locate data points that are in the vicinity.

1.2 Approximate Match

With this type of shape retrieval we are interested in answering the query *"find all shapes in a set of shapes that are similar to the query object"*. Approximate matches for a given query shape are database shapes that are similar, though not necessarily identical, to the query shape. Of course, shapes that satisfy some dissimilarity measure can also be retrieved. There are many notions of similarity which depend on the application domain. The application domain or the user may specify and describe the properties of the notion of similarity. For example, a property might be the invariance of similarity of objects under some kind of transformation such as scaling and rotation. Approximate match searches are likely to be practical for many applications due to many reasons inherited in image processing. For example, due to noise or distortion two fairly similar shapes my have very different descriptions.

Approximate matches are also point searches in the multidimensional index structures. However, to be able to retrieve objects of similar shape, instead of searching one point in the index structures we search for a set of points specified by a range along each index dimension. This has the same effect as blurring the query point that provides some flexibility with regard to the full match. The extent of this blurring can be determined independently for each index dimension, by means of appropriate parameters. The larger the amount of blurring permitted, the weaker the search criteria, and the larger the set of objects selected as being " *similar"* to the given query shape. Thus, approximate match queries translate to range searches on the index. While less efficient than full match queries, most point access methods are designed to perform relatively well on such searches. PAMs do tend to cluster points in close proximity in the n-dimensional space into the same areas of the index structure. A good match of a query point are points in the index whose similarity (i.e., distance) with the query point is less than some threshold value.

1.3   Match with a Specified Transformation

With this type of shape retrieval we are interested in answering the query *"find all shapes in a set of shapes that are exactly identical to the query shape with a specified size and/or orientation"*. With this query type, we investigate whether two shapes are identical with a specified rotation angle, scaling factor, translation vector, or any combination of the three. In some application domains, the support of such query types is important. An example is, searching for similar tumor shapes in a medical image database [46]. Tumors are presented by a set of 2D images that represent slices through it. A method for retrieving similar tumor shapes would help to discover correlations between tumor shape and certain diseases. Besides the shape, the size and the location of the tumor would help in the identification of patients with similar health history. Queries with a specified transformation can be handled in different ways. For example, the transformation parameters (scale, rotation, and translation) are simply real values, so they may be used as part of the multidimensional key and taken into account during indexing.

1.4 Match with Unspecified Transformation

With this type of shape retrieval we are interested in answering the query *"find all shapes in a set of shapes that are exactly identical to the query shape regardless of its size and orientation"*. With this query type, we investigate whether two shapes are identical but are rotation, scaling or translation invariant. Usually, when we think of what a shape looks like, we do not care about the position of the shape in any coordinate system. As such, we would like to retrieve similar shapes from the database irrespective of their positions in the coordinate system used to describe them. In addition, often, besides not caring about the position of the shape, we may not care about the size either. For example, the size may depend on how far the shape was from the camera, or what scale factor is used for the representation. Occasionally we may also wish to permit different scaling along different shape dimensions, rather than the uniform scaling that we normally expect. Such scaling may occur, for example if a picture is taken at an angle to the shape.

Retrieval with such a match can be performed by transforming scale factors from the coordinates of the point, and make the query region as infinite ranges around the point. The query region obtained can then be used as a key in an index search, which retrieves data points that match in all dimensions.

1.5 Partial Match

With this type of shape retrieval we are interested in answering the query *"find all shapes in a set of shapes that are partially similar to a given query shape"*. With this query type, we are interested in finding shapes with components/features matching a (possibly incompletely specified) query shape. The human similarity includes some kind of semantic similarity which considers two parts to be similar if both parts have certain characteristics. In most cases, the characteristics are partial similarities, which means that there exists portions of the two shapes which are similar.

2.   2D Similarity Queries with MBC

This section describes three alternative matching query types that utilize different subsets of the *MBC* features [85]. Those features can be used for both indexing the objects and expediting the comparison between two objects [84, 85]. The three matching query types that utilize different subsets of the MBC features are :

1 With the first query type, we investigate whether two objects are exactly identical in shape (termed, **EM**).

2 With the second query type, we investigate whether two objects are identical in shape but are rotation, scaling, and translation invariant (termed $I\text{-}RST$) or identical objects with a specified rotation angle (R), scaling factor (S), translation vector (T), or any combination of the three $(S\text{-}RST)$.

3 With the third query type, we investigate whether two objects are similar in shape per our definition of similarity (termed, **SIM**).

Therefore, for different query types, different MBC features are used to support the query. Later in Chapter 7, we describe three index structures on different subsets of object's MBC features in order to expedite these query types. For the remainder of this section we explain each query type in more detail.

2.1   Exact Match Shape Retrieval – EM

With this type of object retrieval we are interested in answering the query *"find all objects in a set of objects that are exactly identical to the query object"*. Two objects are identical if they have the same orientation, size, number of vertices and edges, and the exact same dimensions. Some necessary conditions (but not sufficient) for two objects to be identical are:

1 They should have the same number of vertices (m).

2 They should have the same number of touch points (n_{TP}). The number of touch points of an object depends on its MBC. MBC of an object is unique.

3 They should have identical $TPAS$.

4 They should have identical SP.

5 Their $MBCs$ should be of the same size with identical radii.

6 The coordinates for the center C of their MBC's should be identical.

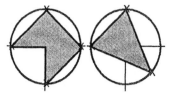
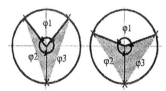

(a): Objects with different number of *TPs*

(b): Objects with the same number of *TPs* but different *TPASs*

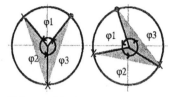
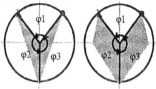

(c): Objects with the same number of *TPs* and the same *TPASs* but with different *SPs*.

(d): Different objects with the same number of *TPs*, the same *TPASs*, and the same *SPs*.

Figure 5.1. MBC touch points TPs; denoted by X; and start point SPs; denoted by bullets

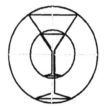

(a): Original object and its uniform scaled version

(b): Original object with its rotated version

(c): Original object with its scaled and rotated version

Figure 5.2. Objects considered identical under **RST** queries

Figure 5.1 shows some examples of objects with identical size of MBC's, but with different n_{TP}, different AS, or different SP.

2.2 RST Shape Retrieval

With this type of object retrieval we are interested in answering two types of queries:

- *"find all objects in a set of objects that are exactly identical to the query object regardless of its size and orientation"* (*I-RST* query type).

- *"find all objects in a set of objects that are exactly identical to the query object with a specified size and/or orientation"* (*S-RST* query type).

We now consider each query in turn. For *I-RST*, it is important that the matching objects be invariant with respect to translation, rotation and scaling. To support the *I-RST* queries, we use those *MBC* features of polygons that are translation, scaling and rotation independent. These are *AS*, either *TPAS* or *VAS*, and n_{TP}. See Figure 5.2, for examples of objects that match with uniform scaling, rotation, and combination of uniform scaling and rotation. Two objects are identical if they meet some necessary conditions; that is they should have: the same number of vertices, the same n_{TP}, and identical *AS*. For *S-RST*, it is important that the matching objects be within a specified rotation angle, scaling factor, translation vector, or any combination of the three. We use object's *SP* to check if it is rotated, use object's r to check if it is scaled, and the vertex coordinates of the object's C to check if it is translated. The description of *I-RST* is straightforward, hence we will only discuss the details for answering *S-RST* query type. Consequently, we consider four different types of exact match queries:

- **Exact Match with Uniform Scaling** With this type of query, we are interested in retrieving all the objects that exactly match our query object but might be at different scales. Hence, the retrieved objects should have the same number of vertices, n_{TP}, *AS*, *SP*, coordinates of centers C of *MBCs* as the query object O^q but might have different radii r.

  When applying uniform scaling to an object, we are only changing its size and not its shape (see Figure 5.3-(a)). Hence, the new scaled object will have the same number of *TP* as the original object. These *TP* are on the extension of the vectors connecting the center of the old *MBC* and the old *TP*. Therefore, the new object's *AS* is equivalent to the old object's *AS* (see Figure 5.3-(b)). Since the distance between a touch point and the center of the *MBC* defines the radius r of the *MBC*, therefore the radius of the scaled *MBC* $r\prime$ should be equal to ar (where a is the scaling factor). From the above discussion, we can conclude that scaling does not change the angle sequence *AS* of an object. The same discussion applies when we represent the object by its *VAS*.

(a): Original object with its scaled version and their *MBCs*

(b): The *TPASs* of both objects: $\langle \varphi_1, \varphi_2, \varphi_3, \varphi_4 \rangle$ and $\langle \varphi'_1, \varphi'_2, \varphi'_3, \varphi'_4 \rangle$

Figure 5.3. MBCs, TPs, and TPASs of an object and its scaled version

- **Exact Match with Rotation** With this type of query, we are interested in retrieving all objects that exactly match our O^q but might be rotated. Hence, the retrieved objects should have the same number of vertices, the same n_{TP}, AS, coordinates of centers C of $MBCs$ and the same $MBC's$ radii as the O^q but might have different SPs. Given the set of candidate objects for exact match, we could find out how much the O^q is rotated by using their SPs. If the coordinates of SPs of the query and the matched objects are (x, y) and (x', y') respectively, then the rotation angle φ could be computed by $\cos \varphi = \frac{xx' + yy'}{\sqrt{x^2 + y^2} \sqrt{x'^2 + y'^2}}$. To determine the direction of the rotation we compute $x'' = x \cos \varphi - y \sin \varphi$ and $y'' = x \sin \varphi + y \cos \varphi$. Since $0 \leq \varphi \leq \pi$, then the point $(x'', y'') = (x', y')$ implies that we have a counterclockwise rotation. Otherwise, (*i.e.* the point $(x'', y'') \neq (x', y')$) we have a clockwise rotation. Note that the same discussion applies when we represent the object by its VAS.

- **Exact Match with Uniform Translation** With this type of queries we look for the objects that have shapes identical to that of O^q without caring about the position of their vertices in the local coordinate system used to describe them (*e.g.* the same object appears in different positions in a plane). Hence, the retrieved objects should have the same number of vertices, the same n_{TP}, AS, $MBC's$ radii, and the same SP as the O^q but might have different coordinates for centers C of $MBCs$. With our model, we can retrieve objects with identical shapes from the database

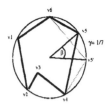

Figure 5.4. β and γ factors

regardless of their positions in the coordinate system. This in-dependence is achieved by representing the objects by their ASs (which is independent of the local coordinate system).

Given the set of candidate objects for exact match, we could find out how much the O^q is translated by using the coordinates of the centers C of their MBCs. If the coordinates of C of the query and the matched objects are (C_x, C_y) and (C_x', C_y') respectively, then the translation vector $\vec{T} = (T_x, T_y)$ could be computed by $T_x = C_x' - C_x$ and $T_y = C_y' - C_y$. Note that the same discussion applies when we represent the object by its VAS.

- **Exact Match with Uniform Scaling, Rotation, and Trans-lation (RST)** This method of retrieval is just a combination of the above three methods. Therefore, we could retrieve exact match objects even if they were scaled, rotated, and translated versions of the O^q. We could also specify the scale factor by using the radius factors of the MBCs, specify the rotation factor by using the angle between the SP points of the objects, and specify the translation vector as the difference between the coordinates C of the MBCs of the objects.

2.3   Similarity Shape Retrieval – SIM

With this type of object retrieval we are interested in answering the query *"find all objects in a set of objects that are similar to the query object"*. There are many notions of similarity which depend on the ap-plication domain. The application domain or the user may specify and describe the properties of the notion of similarity. For example, a prop-erty might be the invariance of similarity of objects under some kind of transformation such as scaling and rotation. This type of notation can be supported by our **RST** query types. Our notion of similarity is that two objects are considered similar if the difference between their VASs is within a specified error margin; this error depends on two parameters β, and γ. Where γ is the percentage of the vertices of the original object that were changed, and β is the percentage of change in the angle of the vector connecting the center of the MBC of the object to one of the object's vertices (see Figure 5.4). Note that our similarity search is also scaling, rotation, and translation invariant; since we are using VAS as a measure of similarity.

Chapter 6

SPATIAL QUERIES

2D Spatial Queries in the World of Minimum Bounding Circles

Introduction

This chapter presents the techniques used to answer spatial queries based on minimum bounding rectangle (MBR) approximation of objects, and how it could be extended for minimum bounding circles (MBC) approximations.

In [64] topological relations between objects are studied based on their minimum bounding rectangles (MBRs). In [25, 63, 66], direction relations between objects are also studied based on MBRs. All of the studies based on MBR of objects use *R-tree* index structure to store and manage the MBRs. They describe the direction relations between objects based on either the *projection-based* method [25, 63], or *cone-directions* method [66].. For this book, since we investigate shape retrieval based on MBC, we also utilize the MBCs to answer spatial queries. We use *Sphere-tree* [57] (which is an indexing technique based on MBCs) to store and manage the objects' MBC approximations. Therefore, we will describe how to support spatial queries such as topological and direction relations between objects using their MBCs [70]. We also show the similarities and differences between approximating objects by their MBR and MBC.

1. Spatial Queries with MBC

In a spatial database system, objects are organized and accessed using spatial access methods (SAMs). Since SAMs are not able to organize complex polygon objects directly, a common strategy is to store objects' approximations. Consequently, those approximations are used to access the spatial data structures. Approximations maintain the most important features of the objects. Therefore, spatial queries can be efficiently processed on the basis of approximations. However, spatial relations (*e.g.*, topological, direction, and distance) between approximations do not necessarily coincide with the spatial relations between the actual objects. In most cases, if the approximations of the actual objects satisfy a given spatial relation, the actual objects may satisfy a number of possible spatial relations (see Figures 6.2 and 6.3). Therefore, if the spatial relations of interest cannot be determined by using the approximations, then the original objects would have to be loaded into memory. Subsequently, complex geometric algorithms would be employed to determine the exact relations. For example, suppose the topological relation of interest is whether two objects *meet* or not. If the approximations of these two objects do not share *common points*, we can conclude that the objects do not *meet*. On the other hand, if the approximations of these two objects have *common points*, no conclusion can be immediately drawn about the topological relation between the actual objects (*i.e.*, the actual objects might meet, overlap,...etc.).

In general, the approximation-based spatial query processing is performed in two steps. First, a *filter step* identifies, based on approximations, a set of the objects that could satisfy the query (*candidate set*). The *candidate set* may contain objects that do not satisfy the query (i.e. *false hits*). Therefore, a *refinement step* is required to inspect the exact representation of each object of the *candidate set* and eliminate the *false hits*. In this step, complex and CPU-time intensive geometric algorithms are used to detect and eliminate the *false hits*. The strategy could also be extended to include more filter steps with finer approximations in order to exclude more false hits from the *candidate set*. If the relations between the objects are unambiguously determined by examining the spatial relations between the approximations of the objects, the refinement step could be completely avoided.

Topological, direction, and approximate distance relations between two objects are examples of spatial relations. A sample spatial composition incorporating topological, direction and distance features is shown in Figure 6.1. It depicts two objects p and q that are *disjoint*, q is *Weak_North_East* of p, and the minimum Euclidean distance between them is bounded by d. For this work, distance relations will not be discussed any further.

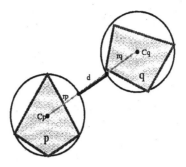

Figure 6.1. Topological, direction, and distance features

The performance of approximation-based query processing depends on the type of approximation used. A suitable approximation is crucial for reducing the size of the candidate set (i.e. reducing the number of false hits). *MBR* as approximation has been studied extensively in the literature. Several other approaches have been suggested to maintain non-rectangular approximations by adequate spatial access methods, *e.g.* circles in the *Sphere-tree*, or convex polygons in the *Cell-tree*, *Polyhedra-tree* or *P-tree*. Here, we focus on *MBC* as approximation and in Sections 2 and 3, we explain how *MBC*s can be employed to approximate topological and direction relations between two objects. We identify the topological and direction information that *MBC*s convey about the actual objects they enclose with respect to the *9-intersection* model [19, 64]. In addition, we discuss how *Sphere-trees* can be utilized to index *MBC*s to expedite spatial queries. The spatial relations between objects based on the minimum bounding rectangles (*MBR*s) approximation as described in [64, 92] are summarized in Appendix 2.

2. Topological Relations

Topological relations are described based on the intersection of the objects topological interiors, boundaries, and exteriors. They are crucial for describing the concepts of neighborhood, inclusion and incidence [64].

Although approximations maintain the most important features of the objects, topological relations between approximations do not necessarily coincide with the topological relations between the actual objects. For example, if two *MBC*s meet, then the relation between their actual objects might be either *meet* or *disjoint* (see Figure 6.2(b)). Moreover,

different approximations of objects would lead to different sets of topological relations that could be deducted between the objects. When approximating objects by $MBRs$, the topological relations between $MBRs$
are determined by the relation between the lower and upper points of
the bounding rectangles of the objects. On the other hand, when approximating objects by MBC, the topological relations between objects
are determined by the relation between the radius and the center of the
bounding circles of the objects. For example, with MBR approximation, if MBR of *p equals* the MBR of q, then the relation between p
and q could be : *equal, covered_by, overlap, cover, meet,* or *disjoint*.
While with MBC approximation, the relation between p and q could be
the same as for MBR except that it cannot be *disjoint*. In general, we
could classify the relations between $MBRs$ as follows:

- Intersect at no point (*i.e.*, represents the topological relations inside or disjoint).

- Intersect at one point (represents meet).

- Intersect at two points (represents overlap).

- Intersect at a line (represents meet or cover).

- Equal (represents equal).

and with MBC we get different relations as follows:

- Intersect at no point (represents inside or disjoint).

- Intersect at one point (represents meet or cover).

- Intersect at two points (represents overlap).

- Equal (represents equal).

Therefore, we need to describe those relations that $MBCs$ could convey about their corresponding objects (see Figures 6.2 and 6.3). Those
relations can also be expressed with the following rules, where $p\prime$ and $q\prime$
are $MBCs$ of p and q, respectively (*eq*: *equal*, *cv*: *cover*, *cb*: *covered_by*,
ct: *contain*, *in*: *inside*, *dj*: *disjoint*, *mt*: *meet*, *ol*: *overlap*):

- $disjoint(p\prime, q\prime) \longrightarrow dj(p, q)$
- $meet(p\prime, q\prime) \longrightarrow dj(p, q) \vee mt(p, q)$
- $overlap(p\prime, q\prime) \longrightarrow dj(p, q) \vee mt(p, q) \vee ol(p, q) \vee ct(p, q) \vee cv(p, q) \vee in(p, q) \vee cb(p, q)$

- $cover(p\prime, q\prime) \longrightarrow dj(p,q) \lor mt(p,q) \lor ol(p,q) \lor ct(p,q) \lor cv(p,q)$

- $covered\_by(p\prime, q\prime) \longrightarrow dj(p,q) \lor mt(p,q) \lor ol(p,q) \lor in(p,q) \lor cb(p,q)$

- $contain(p\prime, q\prime) \longrightarrow dj(p,q) \lor mt(p,q) \lor ol(p,q) \lor ct(p,q) \lor cv(p,q)$

- $inside(p\prime, q\prime) \longrightarrow dj(p,q) \lor mt(p,q) \lor ol(p,q) \lor in(p,q) \lor cb(p,q)$

- $equal(p\prime, q\prime) \longrightarrow mt(p,q) \lor ol(p,q) \lor cb(p,q) \lor cv(p,q) \lor eq(p,q)$

This section studies the topological information that MBCs convey about the actual objects they enclose with respect to the 9-*intersection* model [19, 64]. We also investigate the possible topological relations between MBCs and the corresponding topological relations between the actual objects that they approximate.

When the topological relation between approximations is *overlap* (see Figure 6.2(c)), the number of possible topological relations between the actual objects is large; hence, leads to a large number of false hits. Therefore, we define some special case that depends on the topological relations between MBCs (*e.g.* overlap relations). For the case where the MBCs of the objects *overlap*, we can have more information about the actual objects by knowing the relation between the centers and radii of the MBCs. Furthermore, we define a feature that could be extracted from MBC of an object to classify it as *half-filled* or *fully-filled*. Consequently, those special cases and features are used to reduce the number of *false hits* of the filter step of approximate-based topological relation query processing.

2.1 Topological Relations using MBC

In order to retrieve objects that satisfy a particular relation with q, we need to know what relation exists between the MBC of q and the MBC of those objects. For instance, in order to answer the query *"find all objects that contain object q"*, the *candidate* MBCs are those that satisfy the relations *contain, cover* or *overlap* with the MBC of q. Table 6.1, lists all of the possible topological queries and the possible relations between their corresponding *candidate* MBCs.

In Figures 6.2 and 6.3, we present all possible relations between actual objects when their MBCs are related by one of the 8 possible relations between MBCs. Some relations between MBCs may identify few relations between the actual objects, while other relations between MBCs may identify more relations between the actual objects. For example, if two MBCs meet, then the relation between the actual objects is either *meet* or *disjoint* (see Figure 6.2(b)). On the other hand, if two MBCs

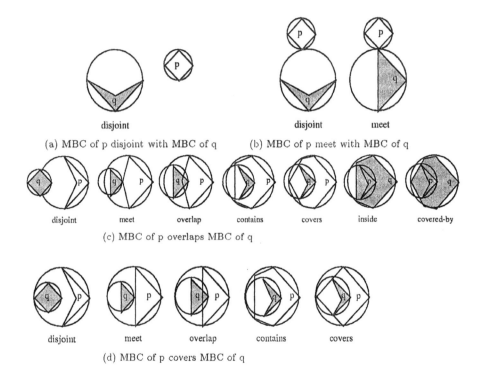

Figure 6.2.   Possible relations between actual objects given the relation between their MBCs

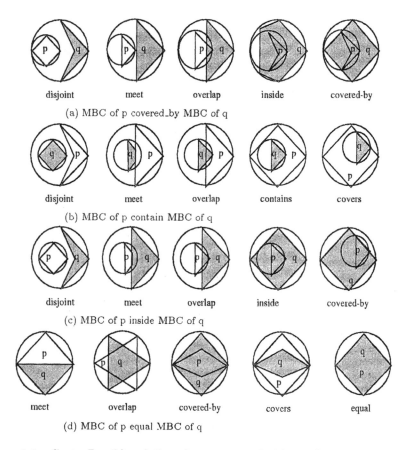

Figure 6.3. Cont. Possible relations between actual objects given the relation between their MBCs

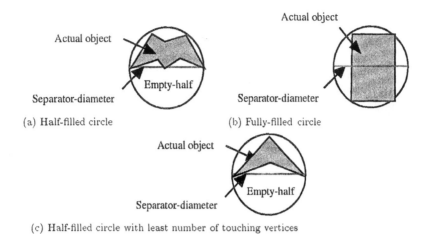

(a) Half-filled circle

(b) Fully-filled circle

(c) Half-filled circle with least number of touching vertices

Figure 6.4.   Half and fully filled circles

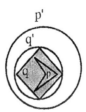

p׳ contain *q׳* and p is inside q

Figure 6.5.   Relations cannot be identified between actual objects given the MBC relations

are equal, then the relation between the actual objects could be *meet*, *overlap*, *covered_by*, *cover*, or *equal*.

To answer a query about objects that have a particular relation with the query object, we need to find the set of *candidate MBC*s. This set contains *MBC*s that satisfy a particular relation with the *MBC* of the query object (see cases in Figures 6.2 and 6.2). Only those *MBC*s could include objects that could satisfy the query. For instance, in order to answer the query *"find all objects that contain object q"*, the *candidate MBC*s would be those that satisfy the relations *contain*, *cover* or *overlap* the *MBC* of the *q*. However, *candidate MBC*s, may also satisfy other relations. For example, to answer the query *"find all objects p equal to object q"*, the only *candidate MBC*s are those that satisfy the relation *equal*. On the other hand, those *candidate MBC*s may also enclose objects that satisfy the relations *meet*, *overlap*, *covered_by* or *cover* with respect to *q* (see Figure 6.3(d)). Therefore, a refinement step is required if the *candidate MBC*s are not *disjoint*.

Sometimes by knowing the relation between the *MBC*s of objects, one could deduce what relations between the actual objects could **not** be satisfied. For example, Figure 6.5 depicts *MBC p/ contain MBC q/*. Consequently, one can deduce that *p* cannot be *inside q* because if *p* is *inside q*, then *p/* cannot be the *MBC* of *p*.

2.2 Special Cases of Topological Relations

There are some special cases, in which we could utilize the topological relations between *MBC*s to reduce the number of false hits from the filter step. We define two such cases, where in the first case we use the information provided by knowing what class of *overlap* the relation between *MBC*s belongs to (see Figure 6.6 for classes of overlap). For instance, if *MBC*s *p/* and *q/* are as in Figure 6.6(overlap-a), then the actual objects *p* and *q* cannot satisfy the relations *contain*, *inside*, *cover* and *covered_by* (see Table 6.2 for other configurations). For the second case, if the two *MBC*s are equal we examine if *MBC*s of the objects are *half-filled* or *fully-filled* (see Definitions 1.6 and 1.7 in Chapter 3). For instance, in the case where the *MBC*s of the objects are *equal* and given that *MBC p/* is *half-filled* and *MBC q/* is *fully-filled*, then object *p* cannot satisfy the relations *cover*(*p*, *q*) or *equal*(*p*, *q*) (see Table 6.3 for other configurations). The two cases are discussed in detail as shown in the following Sections.

Table 6.1.   Queries and the candidate MBCs to answer them

The query to be answered	The relations that the retrieved MBCs must satisfy
"find all objects p *eq* to object q"	$eq(p\prime, q\prime)$
"find all objects p that *contain* object q"	$ct(p\prime, q\prime) \lor cv(p\prime, q\prime) \lor ol(p\prime, q\prime)$
"find all objects p *inside* object q"	$in(p\prime, q\prime) \lor cb(p\prime, q\prime) \lor ol(p\prime, q\prime)$
"find all objects p that *cover* object q"	$ct(p\prime, q\prime) \lor cv(p\prime, q\prime) \lor$ $eq(p\prime, q\prime) \lor ol(p\prime, q\prime)$
"find all objects p *covered_by* object q"	$in(p\prime, q\prime) \lor cb(p\prime, q\prime) \lor$ $eq(p\prime, q\prime) \lor ol(p\prime, q\prime)$
"find all objects p that *overlap* object q"	$cb(p\prime, q\prime) \lor ct(p\prime, q\prime) \lor$ $cv(p\prime, q\prime) \lor in(p\prime, q\prime) \lor$ $eq(p\prime, q\prime) \lor ol(p\prime, q\prime)$
"find all objects p that *meet* object q"	$cb(p\prime, q\prime) \lor ct(p\prime, q\prime) \lor$ $cv(p\prime, q\prime) \lor in(p\prime, q\prime) \lor$ $mt(p\prime, q\prime) \lor eq(p\prime, q\prime) \lor ol(p\prime, q\prime)$
"find all objects p *disjoint* with object q"	$cb(p\prime, q\prime) \lor ct(p\prime, q\prime) \lor$ $cv(p\prime, q\prime) \lor in(p\prime, q\prime) \lor$ $mt(p\prime, q\prime) \lor dj(p\prime, q\prime) \lor ol(p\prime, q\prime)$

eq: equal, cv: cover, cb: covered_by, ct: contain, in: inside, dj: disjoint, mt: meet, ol: overlap

2.2.1   MBCs of objects overlap.

Here, we assume that the relation between MBCs is *overlap*. We can have more information about the actual objects if we knew the relation between the centers of the MBCs. Such relation would be whether each MBC contains the center of the other MBC or not. Figure 6.6 depicts the 9 different cases in which two object's MBCs could overlap, they differ in whether their centers are contained in the MBCs of each other or not. For instance, if MBCs $p\prime$ and $q\prime$ *overlap* but $p\prime$ does not contain the center of $q\prime$ and vice versa (see Figure 6.6(overlap-a)), then the actual objects p and q cannot satisfy the relations *contain*, *inside*, *cover* and *covered_by*.

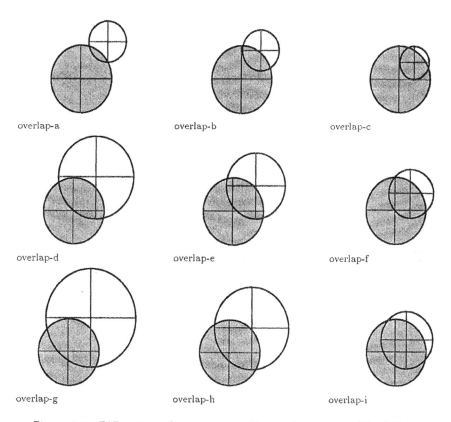

Figure 6.6. Different overlap cases according to the centers of the MBCs

Table 6.2 illustrates the configurations for which the refinement step is not required when the *MBC*s of the objects *overlap*. Each row of the table presents a different type of *overlap* between the *MBC*s of the objects. Each X in a row means that the relation between the actual objects cannot be satisfied according to the heading of the column. For example, in row 3, the relation between *MBC*s is *overlap-c*. Hence, the relations between the actual objects cannot be *contain* but could be *inside*. Therefore, if the relation between *MBC*s is *overlap* then a refinement step is required in some cases, and not in other cases. Figure 6.7 shows some examples where a refinement step is required to identify the relation between the two actual objects. These examples correspond to the cases where the entries in Table 6.2 are blanks. For example, Figure 6.7(a) demonstrates cases where two *MBC*s *overlap* are of type *overlap-g*, *overlap-h*, or *overlap-i* (as defined in Figure 6.6), but we do not know if the actual object p *contain* q or not. On the other hand, there are cases where a refinement step is not required to define the exact relation between the two actual objects. Theorems 1 and 2 define two such cases that correspond to entries in Table 6.2 that are marked by an X. An example is shown in Figure 6.8(a), where two *MBC*s *overlap* of type *overlap-d* and we want to know if the actual object p *contain* q or not.

Theorem 1 *If p overlaps (overlap-d) with q, then the object contained by p cannot contain the object contained by q.*

Proof: Since the overlap is of type *overlap-d*, then the relation between the *MBC*s of p and q should be as shown in Figure 6.7(c). For p to *contain* q, q must be only in the dark shaded area (in Figure 6.7(c)). If q is in the shaded area, then q' is *half-filled* and has only one vertex on the *separator-line* or none. This leads to a contradiction of Lemma 1.8. ∎

Theorem 2 *If p overlaps (overlap-e) with q, then the object contained by p cannot be inside the object contained by q.*

Proof: Since the overlap is of type *overlap-e*, then the relation between the *MBC*s of p and q should be as shown in Figure 6.7(d). For p to be *inside* q, p must be only in the dark shaded area (in Figure 6.7(d)) and has no point on the *separator-diameter*. Thus, p' is *half-filled*

Table 6.2. Configurations for which a refinement step is not required when MBCs of the objects overlap

MBCs overlap	contain(p,q)	inside(p,q)	cover(p,q)	cvd_by(p,q)
Overlap-a	X	X	X	X
Overlap-b	X	X	X	X
Overlap-c	X		X	
Overlap-d	X	X	X	X
Overlap-e	X	X	X	X
Overlap-f	X		X	
Overlap-g		X		X
Overlap-h		X		X

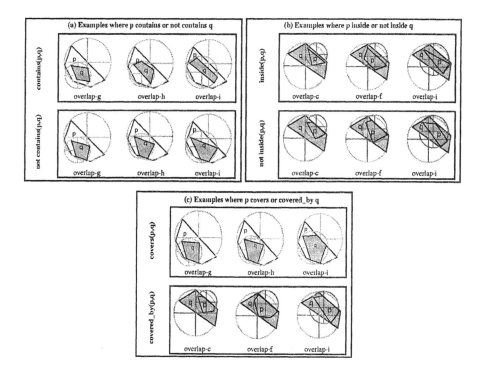

Figure 6.7. Examples where two MBCs are overlapped and a refinement step is required

and has no vertex on the *separator-line*. This leads to a contradiction of Lemma 1.8. ∎

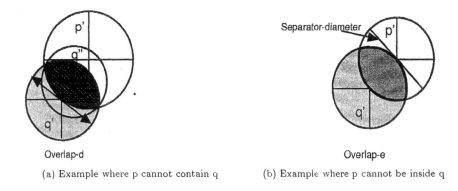

(a) Example where p cannot contain q   (b) Example where p cannot be inside q

Figure 6.8.   Examples in which the two MBCs are overlapped and a refinement step is not required

Table 6.3.   Configurations for which a refinement step is not required when MBCs of the objects are equal

MBCs equal	covered_by(p,q)	cover(p,q)	equal(p,q)
p half-filled, q fully-filled		X	X
p fully-filled, q half-filled	X		X

2.2.2   MBCs of objects are equal.   Here, we describe another way to reduce the number of false hits from the filter step. Suppose the relation between MBCs is *equal*, we can obtain more information about the actual objects if we know whether their MBCs are *half-filled* or *fully-filled* (see Definitions 1.6 and 1.7). Table 6.3 illustrates the configurations for which the refinement step can be entirely eliminated when the MBCs of the objects are *equal*. Each row of the table presents a different type of MBCs. Each X in a row means that the relation between the actual objects cannot be satisfied according to the heading of the column. For instance, in the case where the MBCs of the objects are *equal* and given that the MBC $p\prime$ is *half-filled* and the MBC $q\prime$ is *fully-filled* (row 2), then the object p cannot satisfy the relations $cover(p, q)$ or $equal(p, q)$ (column 2 and 3).

3. Direction Relations

Direction relations describe the order of objects in space (*e.g. north, south*), and are crucial for establishing spatial location and path finding [102]. With *MBR* approximation, a *project-based* method [25, 63] is typically used to define direction relations between objects. With this method a plane is partitioned into some sub-partitions and the direction relation between two objects is defined by the sub-partitions they occupy. This method, however, is not suited when approximating objects with *MBC*. Therefore, we utilize another method named *cone-directions* [66] that could be easily adapted to *MBC*s. With *cone-based*, a plane is divided into 5 partitions that defines the primitive direction relations (see Figure 6.9(d)). Now, it is necessary to investigate what direction relations *MBC*s could convey about their actual objects.

Section 3.1 presents the direction relations between objects based on the concept of *cone-directions*, in which the direction domain is divided into a number of *cones* (or triangles) with a similar resolution (size). We show how the *cone-direction* is well suited for *MBC*s. As the case with topological relation query processing, since we use *MBC* as object approximation to answer the queries, a filter and a refinement step are required. Therefore, we introduce two methods to reduce the number of false hits of the filter step by breaking the *MBC*s of the objects into 4 partitions and further partitioning the *same-level* regions of the objects. Subsequently, the refinement step is needed to eliminate all the false hits produced by the filter step.

3.1 Cone-Based Direction Relations

This section presents the direction relation between objects based on the concept of *cone-directions*. With this concept, the direction domain is divided into a number of *cones* (or triangles) with a similar resolution (size) and a single point q_i is used to represent the *reference* object (q). The cones are consequently used to define the direction relation ; relative to the cone that contains the point p_j, which represents the *primary* object (p). In addition, the direction relation between two objects can be specified more accurately using the angle between a line connecting the objects and a fixed direction in space. For example, in Figure 6.9(a), the direction relation of p relative to q is represented as : p is *north* of q with an angle value of 100 deg. The relation between two points could also be extended to define direction relations between actual

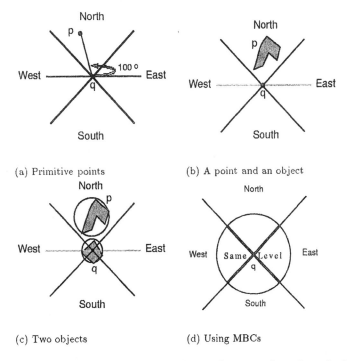

(a) Primitive points   (b) A point and an object

(c) Two objects   (d) Using MBCs

Figure 6.9.   Primitive direction relations using cone-shaped method

objects. We illustrate that by the two examples shown in Figure 6.9(b) and Figure 6.9(c), in which we define the direction relation between a point and an object, and between two objects.

The *cone-based* method could be easily adapted to our representation of objects as $MBCs$. The direction relation between any two objects can be computed by using their $MBCs$ as object representative. We define these relations according to the direction relations in Figure 6.9(d), where the plane is represented by 5 direction partitions. The circle represents the MBC of the *reference* object, the part/s of the primary object that lay *in* the MBC of the *reference* object are considered to be at the *same* level with the reference object.

Some objects could span more than one partition of the 5 direction partitions (see Figure 6.10(a)); for example an object could have parts in the *North* partition and other parts in the *East* partition. In order to define such relations correctly, we define the direction relation between two objects as a permutation from the set {**N: north, S: south , E: east, W: west, SL: same level**}. Therefore, for the objects $p1$, $p2$, $p3$,

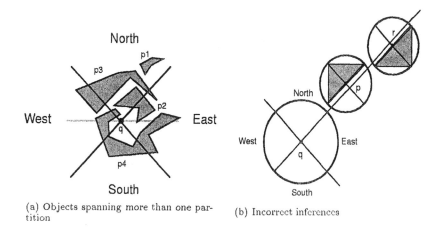

(a) Objects spanning more than one partition

(b) Incorrect inferences

Figure 6.10. Special direction cases

and p4 in Figure 6.10(a) we could define their direction relations with respect to the *reference* q as {N},{N,E},{W,N,E}, and {N,E,S,W}, respectively.

Using *MBC*s as representative for objects when finding the direction relations between objects may lead to incorrect inferences (*i.e.* false hits). For example, in Figure 6.10(b) the direction relation between p and p/ with respect to q is a member of {North,East} but the actual objects do not satisfy these relations (*i.e.*, p satisfies {East} and r satisfies {North}). A naive solution to this problem could be a refinement step which requires the retrieval of the original objects. Our proposed solution, however, is to filter out more false hits in the filter step. We achieve that by dividing the *MBC*s and the *same-level* regions into 4 partitions (see Figure 6.11(a)). For the partitions where the actual object lays in, we assign a 1, otherwise we assign a 0. Subsequently, the direction relation between two objects could be defined by using only the partitions marked 1. For example, in Figure 6.11(b) the direction relation between q and p/ is defined as {N} only and not {N,E}. The same concept could be used for the case of objects at the same level. For instance, in Figure 6.12(c) the direction relation between p and q could be defined more accurately as {North} instead of {North,East,West}.

The definition of direction relations could be extended to define direction relations between 3D objects. In 3D world, we approximate each object by its minimum bounding sphere. Given a point in 3D plane,

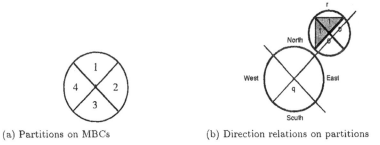

(a) Partitions on MBCs   (b) Direction relations on partitions

Figure 6.11.   Minimum bounding circle partitioning

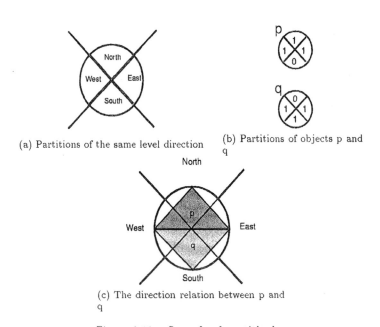

(a) Partitions of the same level direction

(b) Partitions of objects p and q

(c) The direction relation between p and q

Figure 6.12.   Same level partitioning

we define eight direction relation partitions with the reference point as its center (see Figure 6.13). Four of the partitions are considered to be *above* the *reference* point and the other four are considered to be *below* the *reference* point. The following is a list of all direction partitions:

- *partition*1: all points in this partition and its extension (to the outside) are considered to be *Below-Front-Left* of the *reference* point.

- *partition*2: *Below-Front-Right*

- *partition*3: *Below-Back-Right*

- *partition*4: *Below-Back-Left*

- *partition*5: *Above-Front-Left*

- *partition*6: *Above-Front-Right*

- *partition*7: *Above-Back-Right*

- *partition*8: *Above-Back-Left*

All the discussion for the 2-D objects direction relations could be easily extended for 3-D objects. The only difference is that we divide each *MBS* to 9 partitions instead of 5 partitions of *MBC*'s (as for 2-D objects). The *MBS* of the *reference* object is considered as *partition--0*. We divide the rest of the space into 8 different sub-spaces, where each one of them is the extension of the partitions in the *MBS* of the *reference* objects (see Figure 6.14).

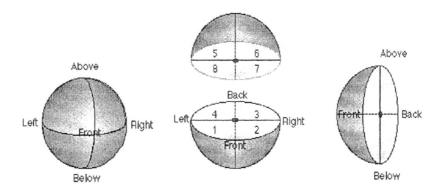

Figure 6.13. Primitive direction relations in 3-D space

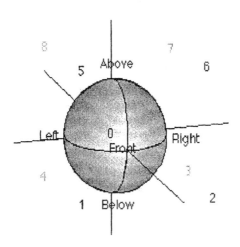

Figure 6.14. Primitive direction relations partitions in 3-D

Chapter 7

MULTIDIMENSIONAL INDEX STRUCTURES

Shape Index Structures

Introduction

As mentioned in Chapters 1 and 3, the shape representation of objects can be used to query and search the object databases for different purposes. For example, CAD/CAM, computer graphics, and multimedia applications try to find objects in a database that match a given object. Besides similarity matching, many other applications in the areas of cartography, computer vision, spatial reasoning, cognitive science, image and multimedia databases, and geographic applications require to represent and process spatial relations between objects. There are two obstacles for efficient execution of such queries. First, the general problem of comparing two 2D objects under rotation, scaling, and translation invariance is known to be computationally expensive [3]. Second, the size of the databases are growing and hence given a query object the matching objects should be retrieved without accessing all the objects in the database. Based on the discussions above we can identify an important basic problem: given a query object, a set of similar objects or objects satisfying some spatial relation should be retrieved without accessing all the objects in the database. Efficient solutions to this problem have important applications in database, image and multimedia information systems as well as other potential application domains. In practice, most retrieval applications (e.g., multimedia applications) involve large databases of images. Such applications could include image databases where the number of objects of interest ranges in the thousands and hundreds of thousands. For large image sets, computational performance cannot be ignored as an issue. When storing the feature vectors in a standard, linear file with one record to each feature vector, we are bound to scan through all feature vectors to find the feature vector most similar to the query feature vector. Linear scanning the feature vector file puts interactive response times out of reach for large data sets of images. Therefore, in order to improve search efficiency, multidimensional index structures (e.g., *R-tree* [39]) were developed. The benefit of indexing over traditional search-based matching schemes is that it does not require considering each feature vector separately. It avoids the need to match the query image with every image in the database, and is thus less dependent on the database size. During index creation, the feature vectors of the images are inserted into a multidimensional index structure (e.g., *R*-tree* [5], *TV-tree* [48], *BANG-File* [26], *k-d-b-trees* [69], or *X-tree* [7]). For processing a similarity query, we transform the query shape into a feature vector, with which we then perform a *k* nearest neighbor query. As a result, we obtain a set of *k* feature vectors having a small Euclidean distance to the query vector. These feature vectors belong to shapes of the database objects having similar properties as the query shape and therefore, are similar to the query shape. Indexing schemes share a uniform underlying structure. They compute *invariants* (features) from an image that are then used as indices. The indices return a list of candidate images with associated weights indicating their likelihood for matching. However, indexing schemes mainly differ in the choice of features (invariants) employed as indices, the way they represent or map the features to the problem space, and the *partitioning* techniques they apply to the problem space (e.g., *space partitioning*, *data partitioning*). In the following sections, we describe the major classes of multidimensional index structures to achieve faster than sequential searching such as *"point access methods"* (*PAMs*) and *"spatial access methods"* (*SAMs*). These are index structures to manage a large collection of multidimensional points (or rectangles or other geometric objects) stored on the disk so that, *"similarity queries"* can be efficiently answered. Similarity queries on such index structures are basically *"range queries"* that specify a region (*e.g.*, *hyper-rectangle* or *hyper-sphere*) in the address space, requesting all the data objects that intersect it. If the data objects are points (as with PAMs), the range query returns all the points that are inside the region of interest. Finally, we provide some definitions of parameters that can be used to evaluate the performance of a given index structure.

1. Point Access Methods (PAMs)

A *point access method* (*PAM*) is a data structure that supports storage and retrieval of points in a multidimensional space. Such structures are typically tree based and support range searches as well as point retrieval. PAMs do tend to cluster points in close proximity in the *n-dimensional* space into the same areas of the index structure. A good match of a query point are points in the index whose similarity with the query point is less than some threshold value. Any multidimensional point access method can be used to organize the objects' shapes to enable efficient search for similar shapes. The stored features of the shapes can be represented as points in a multidimensional space. In addition, each feature/point in the index can be associated with a list which provides information about the shapes that such feature is present in, and the images that contain that shape. To retrieve similar shapes, the index structure is first searched to find the features that are similar (close proximity) to a selected feature of the query shape. Second, the list of shapes associated retrieval systems, such as $BANG - File$ [26], k-d-b-$tree$ [69], $Grid - File$ [56] based methods, $Buddy$-$tree$ [82], $R - tree$ [39] and its variants (R^+-$tree$ [83], R^*-$tree$ [5]), and hB-$trees$ [49].

2. Spatial Access Methods (SAMs)

In point access methods, the objects' shape features are represented as multidimensional point data in space (e.g. images ordered by a multidimensional key). However, some objects are represented by more complex multidimensional features (spatial data) in space (e.g., rectangles or polygons). Therefore, a variety of spatial access methods (SAMs) have been proposed for image retrieval systems [79]. However, since SAMs are not able to organize complex objects (e.g., polygons) directly, a common strategy is to store object approximations and use these approximations to index the data space. Approximations maintain the most important features of the objects (position and extension) and therefore they can be used to efficiently *"estimate"* the result of a spatial query. The advantage of using approximations is that the exact representation of the object is not often required to be loaded into main memory and be examined by expensive and complex computational geometry algorithms. Instead, relationships between the approximations of the objects can be examined quite efficiently. For example, for an efficient storage and retrieval of the two-dimensional feature objects in multidimensional space, we can determine the minimal bounding boxes (MBRs) of the objects in d-dimensional space and store these boxes using a spatial access method (SAM). By using spatial access methods, the problem of finding similar polygons has been reduced to the problem of searching two-dimensional extended feature objects in d-dimensional space. Therefore, a typical technique to improve the performance of spatial queries, is to examine the objects' approximations instead of the actual representations of the objects (typically represented by polygons). The problem, however, is that by using objects' approximations we introduce *false hits*in which the relation between the approximations is a superset of the relations between the actual objects. Thus, a successful approximation is the one that reduces the number of false hits. A recent survey in [79] groups several spatial access methods into the following classes: (a) Methods that transform rectangles into points in a higher dimension space such as *Grid-File* [56]; (b) methods that use *linear quad-trees* [79] or, equivalently, the *"z-ordering"* [59], or other *"space filling curves"* [22, 42]; and finally, (c) methods based on trees (e.g., *k-d-trees* [6], *k-d-b-trees* [69], *hB-trees* [49], *cell-trees* [37], *R-tree* [39], R^+-*tree* [83], and R^*-*tree* [5]). In this section we will focus on the most promising class of methods that are in use on large image databases, which is the last class (methods based on trees).

2.1   The Tree-Based Indexing Methods

A variety of indexing techniques have been proposed for image retrieval systems, of which the most promising appear to be the multidimensional *tree-based* indexing methods (e.g., *R-tree* family [5, 39]). The tree-based methods can be broken into three classes based on the partitioning techniques applied: space partitioning, data partitioning, and distance-based techniques [88].

Space Partitioning Indexing Techniques. *"In space partitioning index techniques, the feature space is organized like a tree. A node in this tree stands for a region in this space. When the number of points in a region exceeds a prescribed amount, the region is split into subregions which become the children of the node containing the original region"* [88]. The best known indices in this class are the k-d-*tree* [6], k-d-b-*tree* [69], ϵ k-d-b-*tree* [87], and hB-*tree* [49].

Data Partitioning Indexing Techniques. *"Data partitioning index techniques associate, with each point in feature space, a region that represents the neighborhood of that vector"* [88]. These techniques are based on the observation that real data in high-dimensional space are highly correlated and clustered, and therefore the data occupy only some sub-space of the high-dimensional space. An R-tree [39] is such a data partitioning structure to index hyperrectangular regions in n-dimensional space. The leaf nodes of an *R-tree* represent the minimum bounding rectangles of sets of feature vectors. An internal node is a rectangle encompassing the rectangles of all its children. The best known indices in this class are the *M-tree* [16], R^+-*tree* [83] , R^x-*tree* [5], *SS-tree* [98], SS^+-*tree* [47], *SR-tree* [43], and *X-tree* [7].

Distance-based Indexing Structures. *"Distance-based index structures are example-based space-partitioning techniques, and hence, very suited for query by example when feature space is metric. The primary idea is to pick an example point and divide the rest of the feature space into groups in concentric rings around the example"* [88]. SAMs assume that comparison of feature values is a trivial operation with respect to the cost of accessing a disk page, which is not always the case in multimedia application. Therefore, distance-based index structures have been designed to reduce the number of distance computations required to answer a query. *MVP-tree* [11] is an example of a distance-based index. It generalizes the vantage point tree (VP-tree) for high dimensional feature vectors. The *MVP-tree* is a static data structure that uses multiple example (*vantage*) points at each node. The first vantage point is used to create partitions. And in each partition, a second vantage point creates more divisions. The best known indices in this class are *metric trees* (e.g., *M-tree* [16]). *Metric trees* only consider relative distances of objects (rather than their absolute positions in a multi-dimensional space) to organize and partition the search space, and just require that the function used to measure the distance (dissimilarity) between objects to be metric.

2.2   Index Evaluation Parameters

The work in [87] provides some guidelines and parameters that can be used to measure the performance of different multidimensional index structures. In this section, we provide the formal definitions of such parameters.

Number of Neighboring leaf Nodes. Measures the increase in the number of neighboring leaf nodes within at most an epsilon-distance of a given leaf node with the number of dimensions. This increase is related to the splitting algorithms used by the different index structures, and the number of dimensions utilized by the splitting algorithm. Splitting algorithms are the criteria used to choose the sub-tree to insert the new data, and used to reduce overlapping between the nodes.

Storage Utilization. Measures the space needed to store the representation of the objects or their approximations/bounding regions (e.g., Minimum bounding rectangles, MBR), and studies how the size of the index structures increases as the dimension of the problem increases.

Traversal Cost. Measures the overhead of the CPU cost examining bounding regions of children in a node of a tree (to determine whether to traverse the sub-tree branching from the children or not) in proportion to the number of dimensions of data points.

Build Time. Measures the cost to build a spatial index on-the-fly. The set of objects participation in a spatial join may often be pruned be selection predicates. In those cases, it may be faster to perform the non-spatial selection predicate first (build a new spatial index for them) and then perform spatial join on the result.

Skewed Data. Measures the ability of an index structure in handling skewed data. The growth in the size of the directory structure can become very rapid for skewed high-dimensional points when using index structures that do not have good support for skewed data.

Table 7.1 presents the properties of a variety of indexing techniques used by different image retrieval systems. From Table 7.1 we can conclude that a variety of indexing techniques have been proposed for image retrieval systems, however, each index has advantages and drawbacks. Hence, it is difficult to design a general-purpose multi-dimensional index structure which does not have any of the shortcomings listed above. For example, one of the most promising approaches in the multidimensional data partitioning index techniques are the *R-tree* [39] and its

Table 7.1.   Properties of a set of indexing structures

Index Structure	Increase in Number of Neighboring Leaf Nodes with the Number of Dimensions	Increase in Storage Utilization with the Number of Dimensions	Traversal Cost of Children in a Node	Index Build Time	Handling Skewed Data
$R-tree$	High	Linear	High	High	Good
R^*-tree	High	Linear	High	High	Good
R^+-tree	High	Linear	High	High	Good
$BANG$ File	–			High	Good
$GridFile$		No		High	Bad
$X-tree$	High			High	Good
$TV-tree$	Low	No	Medium	High	Good
$SS-tree$	High			High	Good
$K-D-B-$ tree	High		High	High	Good
$HB-tree$	High	No	Medium	High	Good

derivatives. The major problem with *R-tree*-based index structures is the overlap of the bounding boxes in the directory, which increases with growing dimension. However, in contrast to most other *point access* multidimensional index structures (such as *k-b-d-trees*, *grid files*, and their variants), *R-tree-based* index structures do not need point transformations to store spatial data and therefore provide a better spatial clustering. Another example is that most current spatial access methods are efficient for small dimensional data points (of order 1-10), however, the time and space for these indices grow rapidly with dimensionality. As the data dimensionality increases, the query performance of these structures degrades rapidly. This phenomenon, generally referred to as the *dimensionality curse*. Multidimensional indexing looks unattractive unless ways can be found to reduce the dimensionality of the index space without impairing search efficiency. Many approaches were proposed in the literature to solve the *dimensionality curse*. For example, some techniques such as SVD transformation [94] reduce the dimensionality of the data by condensing most of the information in a data set to a few dimensions by applying *singular value decomposition (SVD)*. The data in the few condensed dimensions are then indexed to support fast retrieval based on shape content. Such a reduction is however accompanied by a loss of precision of query results. Another approach (e.g. *TV-tree* [48]), is based on the observation that in most high-dimensional data sets, a small number of the dimensions bear most of the information. Hence, the *TV-tree* reduces the dimension of the feature vectors by collapsing the first few dimensions with the same values. However, the *TV-tree* suffers from a different problem, it will only use the first k dimension for splitting, and does not consider any of the others (unless many points have the same value in the first k dimensions). With enough data points, this leads to the same problem as for the *R-tree*, though for the opposite reason. Since the *TV-tree* uses only the first k dimensions for splitting, each leaf node will have many neighboring leaf nodes within epsilon-distance.

3.   MBC Index Structures

All six MBC features described in Chapter 3 are stored in the database to expedite the processing of the three query types. From the six MBC features, three are stored only with the object: r, C and SP. The other three are used to index the objects: TP, $TPAS$x$TPAS$, and VASxVAS. We propose three types of index structures on these three MBC features. The first structure, I_{TPAS}, indexes the objects according to their number of vertices (m), n_{TP}, and their $TPAS$s. The second structure, I_{VAS}, uses VAS of the objects for indexing purpose. Finally, the third index structure, I_{TPVAS}, is a hybrid of the first two structures, where it uses the information provided by both the vertices of the objects (VAS and m) and their TPs. For the purpose of comparison, we start by describing a naive index structure, I_{NAIVE}, which only uses objects' m's for indexing purpose. Note that m is not a feature extracted from the MBC of an object. With I_{TPVAS} and I_{VAS}, we only use a few coefficients of Discrete Fourier Transformation-DFT of the angle sequences in order to reduce the dimensions of the index. With the information kept by all the three structures, we can answer both EM and RST query types. However, to support the SIM query type, we need the information on the entire vertex angle sequences as the first (and only) level of the

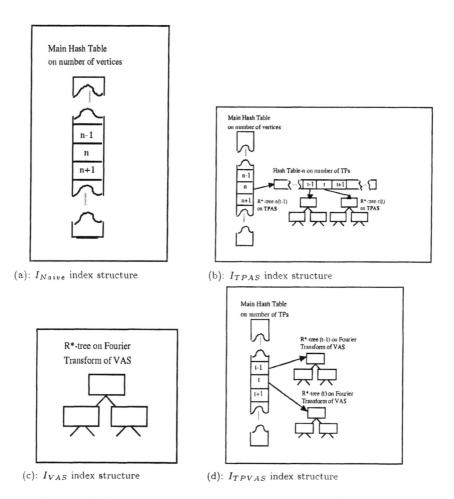

(a): I_{Naive} index structure

(b): I_{TPAS} index structure

(c): I_{VAS} index structure

(d): I_{TPVAS} index structure

Figure 7.1. Index structures I_{Naive}, I_{TPAS}, I_{VAS}, and I_{TPVAS}

index. Therefore, only the I_{VAS} index structure can be used to support the **SIM** query type.

To build an index structure, we use the extracted MBC features for every object in the database. Subsequently, to support a query, the same MBC features are also extracted from the query object O^q. Consequently, O^q's MBC features can be used as a key in searching the index. The index only helps to identify a set of *candidates* that satisfy the query, *i.e.*, we might have false hits but no false drops. This set is then filtered in two steps in order to eliminate all the false hits. In the first step, we use a subset of MBC features that are stored with the object (i.e., SP, r, and C), to identify rotated, scaled and/or translated candidates. Finally, in the last step, the final candidates can be compared to O^q by employing any known algorithm proposed in the area of computational geometry. Instead, we continue utilizing MBC features for the final comparisons. Towards this end, we employ our feature-based comparison algorithms, termed $PCEM$, $PCRST$, and $PCSIM$, which are used for **EM**, **RST**, and **SIM** queries, respectively (see Appendix 2 for further details). Our feature-based comparison algorithms are explained in Sections 3.2, 3.3, and 3.4, and their time complexities are compared to a known computational geometric algorithm in Appendix 2. For the remainder of this section we describe each index structure in more detail. Figure 7.1 provides a graphical representation of these index structures.

3.1 I_{Naive} Index Structure

xI$_{NAIVE}$ The naive index structure is simply a hash table built on objects' m's (see Figure 7.1(a)). To support all three query types, we first identify the number of vertices of the query object O^q, and then access the hash table to retrieve all the objects with the same number of vertices. The returned set of objects from the index, in response to a query, forms the candidate set which trivially contains false hits. To eliminate the false hits, we apply a polygon comparison algorithm PC proposed in [3]. The complexity of the proposed algorithm to compare two objects O^i and O^j is $O(m^{i^8})$; where in our case $m^i = m^j = m$. This computation complexity does not account for examining scaling-invariance, it only checks for translation and rotation invariance.

3.2 I_{TPAS} Index Structure

This index structure uses an object's m, the n_{TP}s and $TPAS$s to construct the index, and can be used to solve the **EM** and **RST** queries (see Figure 7.1(b)). The I_{TPAS} index structure consists of three levels. At the first level, we index the objects according to their m's using a hash table. At the second level, we use a hash table based on their n_{TP}s. Finally, at the third level the objects with the same m and n_{TP} are indexed using a multi-dimensional index structure (R*-tree) according to their $TPAS$. To eliminate false hits, further filtering is done by comparing the final set of objects to O^q to check if they are exactly the same. The overall complexity for **EM** queries using I_{TPAS} index structure is of order $O(m)$, and for **RST** queries is of order $O(n_{TP} \times m^2)$.

Our intuition is that n_{TP} would be a small number greater than 2. With a very large database of objects, we expect that a large number of objects will have identical n_{TP}. Therefore, we index the objects at the second level according to their n_{TP}. Since our index structure depends on $TPAS$, it trivially results in false hits. This is due to the fact that two or more different objects in the database may have the same $TPAS$s.

Query Processing. The I_{TPAS} index structure can be used to solve the **EM** and **RST** queries. For **EM** queries, given a query object O^q we use its number of vertices m^q to access the first hash table to find the objects that have the same number of vertices as m^q. Subsequently, we use its n_{TP}^q to access the second hash table to find the objects that have identical m^q and n_{TP}^q. Finally, we use O^q's $TPAS$ to access the R* tree to find the objects that could be candidates for exact match. Further filtering is done by eliminating objects with different r, coordinates for C, or different SPs. Then the final set of objects could be compared to the query object O^q to check if they are exactly the same. Towards this end, we employ one of our feature-based comparison algorithms, termed $PCEM$. $PCEM$ starts by overlaying each candidate object O^c with the query object. Overlaying means that we have the same MBC centers and we align the SP on top of each other. Then, we have to check the following:

a- The number of vertices between each two consecutive touch points of O^q is the same as the number of vertices between each two consecutive touch points of O^c; this is of order $O(1)$. If not, then they do not match exactly. Otherwise continue with the next step.

b- Find the Euclidean distance between the corresponding vertices of O^q and O^c; this is of order $O(v)$. If the Euclidean distance is close to zero, then the two objects exactly match.

Therefore, the overall complexity for exact match **EM** of polygons using $\mathbf{I_{TPAS}}$ index structure; $O_{EM-TPAS}$; is of order $O(v)$.

For **RST** queries, we follow the same steps taken to support **EM**. The only exception is in the queries that involve rotations. We mentioned in Section 1 that having an object with a different SP leads to a different AS; especially for the rotated objects. Therefore, given a query object, we have to perform n_{TP} queries to find the candidate objects for match. This is due to the fact that we have n_{TP}-different SPs and all of these are considered identical under rotation. Note that this was not the case for **EM** queries, since with **EM** two objects cannot be candidates for exact match if they do not have the same SP. This is due to our choice of the start point. Two objects would be exactly identical; not rotated; if and only if their SPs lay on the same line through the center of MBC (see Figure 5.3(a)).

Further filtering is done by comparing the final set of objects to the query object O^q to check if they are exactly the same. Towards this end, we employ one of our feature-based comparison algorithms, termed $PCRST$. $PCRST$ starts by overlaying each candidate object with the query object. Subsequently, we eliminate the objects with different m. Finally, we check the following:

a- The size of the radii of MBC^q and MBC^c. If they are not the same, then scale up/down the O^q such that $r^q = r^c$; this is of order $O(v)$.

b- Check if the SP of O^q has the same coordinates as the candidate object. If they are not the same, then rotate O^q by θ degrees until its SP is on top of the SP of the candidate object. This is of order $O(n_{TP} \times v)$; since we need to rotate v vertices of O^q n_{TP} times and for each time we do :

    1- Check if the number of vertices between each two consecutive touch points of the O^q is the same as the number of vertices between each two consecutive touch points of the candidates object; this is of order $O(1)$. If not, then they do not match exactly. Otherwise continue with the next steps.

    2- Find the Euclidean distance between the corresponding vertices of O^q and O^c; this is of order $O(v)$. If the Euclidean distance is close to zero, then the two objects exactly match.

Therefore, the overall complexity of **RST** queries using $\mathbf{I_{TPAS}}$ index structure, $O_{RST-TPAS}$, is of order $O(n_{TP} \times v^2)$.

3.3 I_{VAS} Index Structure

xI_{VAS} The I_{VAS} index structure uses the ASs of all the vertices of the objects to construct the index, and can be used to solve the **EM**, **RST** and **SIM** queries. It consists of a single R*-tree on the fourier transform of the VAS of the objects (see Figure 7.1(c)). Experiments [60] have shown that R*-tree based methods work well for up to 20 dimensions. In addition, in [1] they showed that using an $f_c \leq 3$ is more than efficient to index data sequence of sizes larger than 256 elements. Therefore, we use only the first f_c coefficients of the fourier transforms of the VASs to both reduce and fix the dimensionality of the problem. The Euclidean distance between sequences is used as a measure of similarity of two sequences. In [58] Parsevals theorem shows that the Euclidean distance is preserved under orthonormal transforms such as DFT. This would guarantee that we have no false drops, but note that we might produce some false hits.

For the **EM** or **RST** queries, using the fourier transformation of the VAS provides us with extra information. The *real* part of the first fourier coefficient is the summation of all the angles in the angle sequence divided by the square root of the number of angles in the sequence. For our problem, the angles in an angle sequence could be *positive* or *negative* but the summation of the angles in an angle sequence is always equal to 2π. The first coefficient satisfies the equation $Z_0 = 2\pi/\sqrt{nsv}$. Hence, this equation can be used to compute the number of vertices in an object, given the first fourier coefficient of its AS. To eliminate the false hits, further filtering is done by employing our feature-based comparison algorithms. The overall complexity for **EM,RST**, and **SIM** queries using I_{VAS} index structure is of order $O(m)$, $O(m^3)$ and $O(m^3)$, respectively.

Query Processing.   The I_{VAS} index structure can be used to solve the **EM**, **RST** and **SIM** queries. For **EM** queries, given a query object O^q we use its VAS to access the R*-tree to find the objects that could be candidates for exact match. Further filtering is done by employing $PCEM$. We could skip step-(a) but the complexity would still be the same, *i.e.*, $O_{EM-VAS} = O_{EM} = O(v)$.

For **RST** queries, the same steps used to answer **EM** queries would be required here. The only exception is in the queries that involve rotations. We have to to perform k queries to find the candidate objects for match, where k is the number of touch points of the query object. Further filtering is done by employing $PCRST$. We can skip step-(a-1) and for step-(b) the number of rotations would be equal to v. Hence, $O_{RST-VAS}$ would be of order $O(v^3)$.

For **SIM** queries, we have to perform more queries. Since we do not use the touch points information, then any vertex of an object (not only its touch points) could be used as the SP. Therefore, each object would have m different AS representations. Consequently, we have to apply m queries in order to find all the objects that could be similar to the query object. With each of the m queries, we use the same steps required for answering **EM** and **RST** queries. Further filtering is done by employing one of our feature-based comparison algorithms, termed $PCSIM$. $PCSIM$ starts by overlaying each candidate object with the query object. Then, we have to check the following:

a- The size of the radii of MBC^q and MBC^c. If they are not the same, then scale up/down the O^q such that $r^q = r^c$; this is of order $O(v)$.

b- Check if the O^q overlaid with the candidate object has matching VASs. If they are not the same, then rotate the O^q by θ degrees until the vertices are aligned in a way such that the VAS of the objects matches. This is of order $O(v^2)$, and for each time we do :

    − Find the Euclidean distance between the corresponding vertices of O^q and O^c; this is of order $O(v)$. If the Euclidean distance is close to a certain ϵ, then the two objects are similar.

The overall complexity for **SIM** queries using I_{VAS} index structure; $O_{SIM-VAS}$; is of order $O(v^3)$.

3.4 I_{TPVAS} **Index Structure**

This index structure is similar to I_{VAS} index structure except that we use the extra information provided by the same n_{TP}. The I_{TPVAS} index structure could be used to solve the **EM** and **RST** queries. The I_{TPVAS} index structure consists of two levels. In the first level we index the objects according to their n_{TP}. At the second level, we index the objects with the same n_{TP}, using R*-tree (see Figure 7.1(d)). As in I_{VAS} , the R*-tree is built on the first f_c fourier coefficients of the object's VAS. The overall complexity for **EM**, **RST**, and **SIM** queries using I_{TPVAS} index structure is of order $O(m)$ and $O(m^3)$, respectively.

Query Processing.   The I_{TPVAS} index structure could be used to solve the **EM** and **RST** queries. For **EM** queries, we use O^q's n_{TP}

to access the hash table to find the objects that have identical n_{TP} as n_{TP}^q. At the last step, we use O^q's $TPVAS$ to access the $R^\star$ tree to find the objects that could be candidates for exact match. Further filtering is done by employing $PCEM$. We can skip step-(a) but the complexity would still be the same, $O_{EM-TPVAS} = O_{EM} = O(v)$.

For **RST** queries, the same steps used to answer **EM** queries would be required here. The only exception is in the queries that involve rotations. We have to perform k queries to find the candidate objects for match, where k equals n_{TP} of the query object. With each of the k queries, we use the same steps required for answering **EM** queries. Then we use the same steps used in processing of **RST** queries in $\mathbf{I_{TPAS}}$. Further filtering is done by employing $PCRST$. We can skip step-(a-1) and for step-(b) the number of rotations would be equal to v. Therefore, $O_{RST-TPVAS}$ would be of order $O(v^3)$.

III

MBC COMPLEX QUERIES, AND EVALUATION FRAMEWORK

Chapter 8

OBSERVATIONS ON MBC AND MBR APPROACHES

Comparison between MBC and MBR Approaches

Introduction

To expedite the processing of spatial queries, objects could be organized and indexed using the *Sphere-tree* index structure. *Sphere-tree* is a spatial access method used for storing and retrieving objects approximated by their *MBC*s; as opposed to the *R-tree* which is used for objects approximated by their *MBR*s. However, in order to utilize *Sphere-tree* to index *MBC*s we need to address the mismatch between approximation relations and actual relations for intermediate nodes of the tree. Intuitively, since *MBC* approximations of objects are different than their *MBR* approximations; we expected that this would change the rules of propagation in the intermediate nodes of *Sphere-tree* compared to those of *R-tree*. On the contrary, our investigations showed that the relations that may be satisfied between an intermediate node P and $q\prime$ (so that the node be selected for propagation in the *Sphere-tree*) are similar to those relations obtained for the case where *R-tree* was used in [64]. The same results were also obtained when investigating the empty results query optimization (*i.e.* where the result of the query is known to be empty without running the query [64]). These observations are described in detail in Sections 1 and 2.

1. Sphere Index for MBCs

In order to retrieve the spatial relations using *Sphere-trees*, we need to define more general relations to propagate the intermediate nodes (may contain several *MBC*s) of the tree structure. By knowing the spatial relation between the *MBC* of the intermediate node (P) and that of the *reference* object q, one could conclude the possible spatial relations between q and all the *primary* objects contained in P. For instance, the intermediate nodes that could enclose $p\prime$ that *cover* $q\prime$, may satisfy the more general constraint $contain(P, q\prime) \lor cover(P, q\prime)$. Otherwise, the intermediate node would not contain any $p\prime$ that satisfies the relation $cover(p\prime, q\prime)$. Thus all the MBCs inside this intermediate node may be ignored from further search. Following this strategy, the search space is pruned by excluding the intermediate nodes P that do not satisfy the previous constraint. Figure 8.1 provides examples of intermediate nodes (P) that may contain MBCs that *cover* the MBC of q.

In Appendix 2, we included Table B.1 that presents the relations that may be satisfied between an intermediate node P and $q\prime$ of the *reference* object, so that the node be selected for propagation in the tree structure as in [64]. Notice that a similar relation between intermediate nodes and the *reference* object's MBC exists for all the levels of the tree structure. For instance, for the example shown in Figure 8.1, an intermediate node ($P\prime$), which encloses the intermediate node (P) that satisfies the general constraint $contain(P, q\prime) \lor cover(P, q\prime)$; may also satisfy a similar constraint. This can be easily concluded from Table B.1 and is applicable to all topological relations of Figure B.2. The same concept could be applied to direction relations. In order to find all the objects to the *North* of a *reference* object q, we need to retrieve all objects which have non-empty partitions (marked 1) in the *north* partition of the MBC of q. A similar partitioning could be applied to the intermediate nodes of the *Sphere-trees*, and could be used to prune the search space by excluding the intermediate nodes P that do not have non-empty partitions in the *north* partition of the MBC of q.

2.   Complex Queries

Sometimes topological relations could be defined as disjunction of the relations of $mt2$ (lower qualitative resolution). Consider the query *"find all the postal offices in a given county in a map"*. The result should be all the offices that are *inside* or *covered_by* that county. Thus, the interpretation of *in* is *inside* $\lor$ *covered_by*. In general, the MBCs to be retrieved are the union of the MBCs to be retrieved by each of the relations that belong to the disjunction. In some cases (*e.g.* empty results query), the results of a topological relation query could be returned

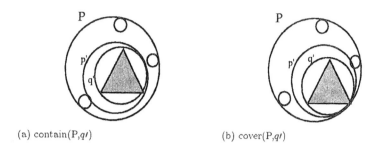

(a) contain(P,$q\prime$)   (b) cover(P,$q\prime$)

Figure 8.1. Intermediate nodes propagation

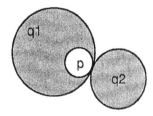

Figure 8.2. A query with two reference objects and empty results

without running the query (semantic query optimization). The empty result is deduced from the relations required in the query between the *reference* object and the *primary* objects. An example of queries of this form is *"find all objects that are covered_by q1 and are inside q2"*. We can determine that the result of this query is empty if we knew that $q1$ *meets* $q2$. As Figure 8.2 illustrates, if p is *covered_by* $q1$ and $q1$ *meets* $q2$, it cannot be the case that p is *inside* $q2$. In Appendix 2, we included Tables B.2 and B.3, that illustrate the relations between *reference* object and *primary* objects for which an empty result is returned without running the query.

Chapter 9

EVALUATION FRAMEWORK

A Framework to Evaluate the Effectiveness of Shape Representation Techniques

Introduction

The shape of an object is an important feature for image and multimedia similarity retrievals, it conforms to the way human beings interpret and interact with the real world objects. The shape representation of objects can therefore be used for their indexing, retrieval, and as a similarity measure. However, as a consequence of uncertainty, shape representation techniques sometimes work well only in certain applications, and their performance highly depends on the quality of the technique used to represent shapes. Therefore, in this chapter, we address key methodological issues for the evaluation of shape retrieval methods with real data and under different scenarios. We describe several metrics and criterions to evaluate and compare the effectiveness and robustness of a given shape retrieval method. The metrics can be used to compare the efficiency of the techniques in terms of: 1) retrieval accuracy in terms of recall and precision, 2) storage cost for their indices, 3) computation cost to generate the shape signature, 4) computation cost to compute the similarity between two different shape signatures, 5) sensitivity to the presence of noise in the database, and 6) sensitivity to the alternative ways of identifying the boundary points of a shape, 7) support for different query types, and 8) impact of human perception. Some ideal features of a shape representation method are: good discriminating capabilities; invariant to scale, translation and rotation; simplicity to extract; low storage and computational cost; robustness. For example, a good shape representation technique should not be dependent on the *edge detection* algorithms and explicit *distinguishable points* (e.g., *corners* or *inflection points*).

1.   Accuracy

In several applications, an important criterion for testing the efficacy of the shape retrieval methods is that for each query object the relevant items (similar shapes) in the database should be retrieved. Therefore, one of the metrics by which we may evaluate a shape representation technique is recall and precision. Recall and precision are commonly used in the information retrieval literature, where recall measures the ability of retrieving relevant shapes in a database and is defined as the ratio between the number of relevant shapes retrieved and the total number of relevant shapes in the database. While, precision measures the retrieval accuracy and is defined as the ratio between the number of relevant shapes retrieved and the number of total shapes retrieved.

To evaluate the accuracy of the alternative shape retrieval methods, the following steps can be followed: First, boundary features (based on shape) are extracted from the objects during the population of the database. Second, for a number of randomly selected query shapes from the database, several similar (relevant) objects can be inserted in the database. The similar objects are variants of the original object constructed as: rotation clockwise/counter-clockwise variants, scaled up/down variants, translated variant, or any combination of them. Consequently, we can simply assume that each shape is relevant only to itself and to its variants. Third, at query time, features are extracted from the query object. Fourth, the query object is compared with the objects in the database on the basis of the closeness of the extracted features. Towards this end, the Euclidean distances between the shape signature of the query object and all other objects' shape signatures are computed. Then, the Euclidean distances are ordered in an ascending order and the system retrieves an ordered list of the relevant shapes from the database in decreasing order of similarity to the query shape. Finally, the accuracy of the retrieval methods can be calculated as precision-recall curve. Towards this end, we identify the ranks of the relevant objects to the query object within the ordered list (according to Euclidean distance). Subsequently, we use 11-point average *precision* at *recall* values of 0%, 10%, 20%,..., 100%, in which we vary the number of items to be returned and compute the precision depending on a required recall value. Note that the retrieval can be done more efficiently using index structures, but since this is not the focus of this work we assumed the sequential scan of the database.

2.   Cost

One metric to evaluate the effectiveness of a shape representation technique is the cost. Cost analysis can compare the efficiency of different shape representation techniques in terms of storage requirement and computation cost during retrieval. Size of databases is growing, therefore it is vital that the shape representation be capable of representing the shapes with minimal storage requirement for their indices. The computation costs of indexing the shapes in the database is usually done off-line. Therefore, we will only concentrate on the computation cost endured during retrieval (query time), which is done on-line. During retrieval, given a query object, methods need to first derive the shape signature for the query and then compare similarity between the query and shapes in the database to retrieve the relevant shapes. Hence, the major operations and required computation cost for a query are: cost to compute the shape signature for the query object, and the cost to compute the similarity between the query object and the objects in the database. Computation cost can be measured by computing the time required to perform each operation (*e.g.*, compute a shape signature), or can be estimated by the number of floating points operations (*i.e.*, the complexity) to perform each operation. The storage cost can be measured as the total capacity (disk space in bytes) required to store the shape signatures of the objects in the database, and the temporary storage required during some of the required comparison operations.

3.   Robustness to Noise

Real data is always accompanied with noise (e.g., by using sensors, scanners, etc.). Hence, when evaluating the efficiency of a shape representation technique, perfect data cannot be expected. In addition, a shape representation technique is expected to be stable and not fail to retrieve a similar shape that is distorted (but not enough to make it different). Therefore, it is necessary to address the issues of robustness/stability of the alternative shape retrieval techniques in the presence of noise.

To evaluate the robustness of the alternative shape retrieval methods, a database of corrupted shapes can be used. Shapes can be corrupted by introducing random *Gaussian noise*, with a specified mean (μ) and standard deviation (σ) (termed $N(\mu, \sigma^2)$), to their vertices. Towards this end, we can consider two different methods for introducing noise to the vertices of a shape. With the first method ($Noise$-$M1$), noise is introduced by adding random samples following Gaussian distribution to the boundary points according to the following approach: if the coordinates of a vertex (k th vertex) of a shape are $(x(k), y(k))$ then the coordinates of the corresponding vertex on the noisy shape $(x_n(k), y_n(k))$ are given by :

$$x_n(k) = x(k) + gn \qquad (9.1)$$
$$y_n(k) = y(k) + gn \qquad (9.2)$$

where gn is a sample from the Gaussian distribution $N(0, 1)$.

With the second method ($Noise$-$M2$), noise is introduced to the shapes following the approach defined in [101] and used in other comparison studies [50, 77]. With this approach, if the coordinates of a vertex (k th vertex) of a shape are $(x(k), y(k))$ then the coordinates of the corresponding vertex on the noisy shape $(x_n(k), y_n(k))$ are given by :

$$x_n(k) = x(k) + d_k \times r \times c \times cos(\theta_k) \qquad (9.3)$$
$$y_n(k) = y(k) + d_k \times r \times c \times sin(\theta_k) \qquad (9.4)$$

where d_k is the distance of boundary point k to point $k+1$, θ_k is the angle from the x-axis to the normal direction of the boundary at point k, r is a sample from the Gaussian distribution $N(0, 1)$, and c is a parameter that controls the amount of distortion. Since our shapes are represented by their boundary vertices (i.e. discrete values), the normal direction of the boundary at point k is approximated by the direction of the vector passing through point k and the midpoint of the line connecting points $k-1$ and $k+1$. Example of a shape and how it is corrupted by introducing different types and values of noise to its vertices was shown in Figure 9.1. Note that as the amount of noise increases, some boundary edges of the shape cross over each other. This cross over leads to different shape signatures of the same object.

4.   Robustness to Boundary Points Selection

For 2D objects, almost all shape representation techniques use the boundary of a shape as its representation. The boundary is usually defined by vertices identified by edge detection algorithms. However, different edge detection algorithms may identify a different number of

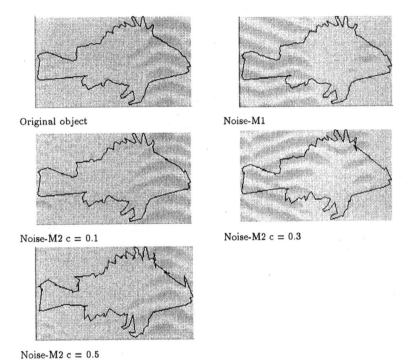

Original object

Noise-M1

Noise-M2 c = 0.1

Noise-M2 c = 0.3

Noise-M2 c = 0.5

Figure 9.1. Example of objects corrupted by Noise-M1 and Noise-M2

vertices for the same shape. In addition, since the boundary is usually defined by a large number of vertices, only a small collection of those vertices (termed *corner points*) is used and serves as the feature points for representing the shape. Consequently, the corner points are used to define the polygonal approximations of the shape. Obviously, the polygon approximation of a shape is not unique and highly depends on the vertices used to represent the shape. Sometimes a shape representation technique may work well only in certain environments, and it's performance may depend crucially on the *edge detection algorithm* used to identify its vertices and on the quality of the technique used to find the *corner points*. For example, with *DT* [90] corner points are defined as *high-curvature* points located along the crossings of an objects' edges. However, a *modified DT* (see *M-DT* in our study [71]), was able to achieve better retrieval performance than that of *DT* due to the use of a different method (i.e., three pass algorithm) to identify corner points.

A good shape representation technique should not be dependent on the edge detection algorithms and explicit distinguishable points (e.g., corners or inflection points). Therefore, it is vital to study the impact of using different polygonal approximations and corner points on the retrieval performance of the alternative shape representation techniques. Towards this end, we propose a new algorithm termed *vertex-reduction* (*VRA*) to be used to identify corner points that represent a shape, and at the same time reduce the number of its vertices. *VRA* strives to reduce the number of vertices required to represent the straight lines in a shapes boundary by using two heuristics to decide when to delete or keep a vertex of a shape boundary: *VRA* algorithm deletes a boundary point of a shape if it meets the conditions described by both of the following two heuristics:

Heuristic-1 The angle (θ) between the vectors (V_{i-1} and V_i) connecting vertex P_i and its two adjacent vertices (i.e., P_{i-1} and P_{i+1}) on the boundary of a shape is less than *Threshold*-1 (see Figure 9.2(a)).

$$\theta(V_{i-1}, V_i) \geq Threshold1$$

Heuristic-2 The length of V_{i-1} (l_{i-1}) compared to the length of V_i (l_i) is less than *Threshold*-2. Moreover, l_{i-1} and l_i are much smaller than l_{i-2} and l_{i+1} (see Figure 9.2-(b)).

Optimally, a straight line could be represented by its two end points. However, typical edge detection algorithms introduce more than two

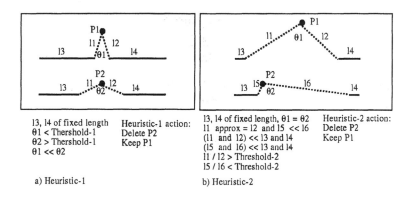

Figure 9.2. VRA algorithm heuristics

points to represent a straight line. The extra points make the straight line look like a jagged line (like saw edge). The intuition behind *VRA*, is that if a vertex (P_i) of a shape satisfies the conditions in both heuristics, then P_i could be deleted without affecting the shape. To represent the same shape with a different number of vertices and corner points, *VRA* could be applied using different threshold values and different numbers of passes of the algorithm. Figures 9.3 and 9.4, show examples of how the *VRA* algorithm identifies the corner points and reduces the number of vertices representing a shape while at the same time it maintains its general characteristics. In Figure 9.3 we apply a one pass *VRA*, while in Figure 9.4 we apply a three pass *VRA*.

5. Support of Different Query Types

A good shape representation technique should be capable of supporting several query types (*i.e.*, similarity and spatial) using the same objects representation. For similarity search, a shape representation technique should be capable of supporting different types of similarity search queries such as: 1) exact match, 2) exact match regardless of its size and orientation (termed *I-RST*), 3) exact match with a specified rotation angle (*R*), scaling factor (*S*), translation vector (*T*), or any combination of the three (*S-RST*). The support for such query types (especially *S-RST*) is essential in some application domains. For example, searching for similar tumor shapes in a medical image database [46]. A tumor is represented by a set of 2D images, each corresponding to a slice cut through its 3D representation. A method for retrieving similar tumor

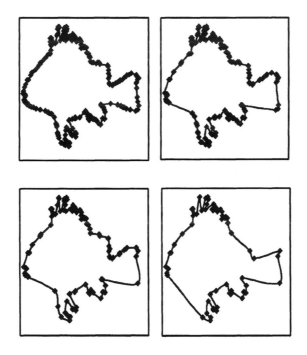

Figure 9.3.   Example of applying 1-pass VRA algorithm

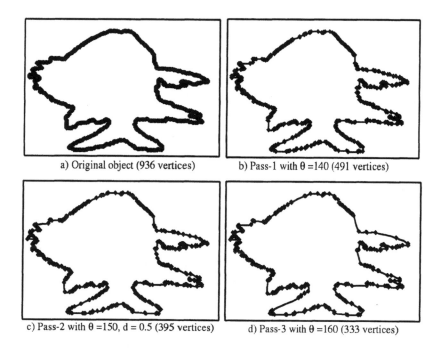

a) Original object (936 vertices)   b) Pass-1 with θ =140 (491 vertices)

c) Pass-2 with θ =150, d = 0.5 (395 vertices)   d) Pass-3 with θ =160 (333 vertices)

Figure 9.4. Example of applying 3-pass VRA algorithm

shapes would help to discover correlations between tumor shape and certain diseases. Besides the shape, the size and the location of the tumor would help in the identification of patients with similar health history. Another essential query type to support is spatial query (i.e., topological or direction query). Given a query object, the shape representation technique should be capable of finding a set of objects satisfying some spatial relationship efficiently.

6.   Human Perception

Most of the studies assume that human beings ignore variations in shapes (i.e. *affine transformations*) for recognition and retrieval purposes. Hence, each shape is relevant only to itself and to its variants (e.g., rotation, or scaling variants). However, since humans are better than computers in extracting semantic information from shapes [90, 91], human perceptions on shape similarity are appreciably different. For example, a human being could identify two shapes from a database to be similar even though they are considered irrelevant by the computer; i.e., their shape signatures derived using a shape representation technique are different. Therefore, it is vital to incorporate human perception in the evaluation of the effectiveness of the shape matching methods. To this end, a system (*e.g.,* Web-based) with a shape database can be implemented, in which a number of query shapes can be selected randomly from the database. Then, the user selects the most similar shapes in the database per query shape. Finally, compare the accuracy of the alternative shape retrieval methods depending on the similarity of the objects returned from the system and the ones picked by humans.

Chapter 10

MBC OPTIMIZATION TECHNIQUES

Optimization Techniques to Improve the Performance of MBC-Based Retrieval Techniques

Introduction

This chapter explains two optimization techniques [74] to further improve the performance of *MBC-based* shape retrieval method in several aspects. First, we propose a more efficient algorithm to identify the minimum bounding circle (*MBC*) of an object, that operates only on a subset of the object's vertices. Second, we propose a new technique to improve the response time of *MBC-based* methods for match queries under specified rotation angles. The technique relies on utilizing the symmetry property of the phase values of the Fourier transform of a real sequence under different rotations. The fundamental observations utilized by our techniques can be adapted and extended to be applicable to other frameworks and application domains.

1. Optimized MBC Computation Algorithm

We start by describing the algorithm used to find the minimum bounding circle (*MBC*) of an object. *MBC* of any finite set of points (*P*) in

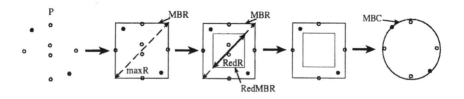

Figure 10.1. Optimized MBC

a 2D plane is their smallest enclosing circle. The set of points P can be divided into two sets P_{in} and P_{on} (touch points); where P_{in} is the set of all points that are contained by the MBC but are not laid on its boundary and P_{on} is the set of all points that are contained by the MBC and are laid on its boundary. To eliminate numerical errors, we use a circle with a wide boundary rather than its line contour. To compute the MBC of an object we use a simple randomized algorithm that computes the smallest enclosing disk (circle) of a set of n points in the plane in expected $O(n)$ (linear time). The algorithm is based on *Seidel*'s Linear Programming, that solves a Linear Program with n constraints and d variables in expected $O(n)$ time, provided d is constant (for details on MBC algorithm see [97]). In general, for a set of n points, the algorithm computes minimum disk containing P in an incremental fashion. It starts with the empty set and adding the points in P one after another while maintaining the smallest enclosing disk of the points considered so far. The expected complexity of the algorithm is independent from the input distribution; it averages over random choices made by the algorithm. In theory, there is no input that should force the algorithm to perform poorly. However, in practical situations, the algorithm sometimes does perform poorly. In [51], another deterministic linear time algorithm for computing smallest enclosing balls was proposed. However, their algorithm is not nearly as easy to describe and to implement as Seidel's algorithm, and it highly depends on the constant d.

In this work, we propose a technique to enhance the performance of the MBC computation algorithm. In [97], a lemma states that if P and R are finite point sets in the plane, and P is nonempty, then if there exists a disk containing P with R on its boundary, the minimum bounding disk of P and R is unique. Therefore, we can conclude that the set of points P_{in} does not affect the MBC algorithm and that P_{on} is the set that uniquely determines $MBC(P)$. In fact, there are at most three points (p) in P_{on} such that $MBC(P)$ is not equal to $MBC(P-p)$; i.e., $MBC(P)$ is determined uniquely by at most three points in P_{on}.

Using the previous observations, we propose a new technique to speed up the MBC computation algorithm by identifying all those points that may belong to P_{in} and compute $MBC(P - P_{in})$. Note that beforehand, given P, we cannot exactly determine P_{on} and P_{in} without actually computing $MBC(P)$. Therefore, we propose an approximation algorithm to find P_{in}. Towards this end, given P, we first compute $MBR(P)$ (in $O(n)$), and identify the largest diagonal of $MBR(P)$ ($maxR$). Second, we compute a reduced (scaled down) MBR ($RedMBR(P)$) with the largest diagonal ($RedR$) equal to $maxR$ reduced by a factor RF (*i.e.*, $RedR = RF \times maxR$). Third, we consider the points inside $RedMBR(P)$ to be P_{in}. Finally, we compute the $MBC'(P - P_{in})$. See Figure 10.1 for a graphical representation of the algorithm. Our approximation algorithm to find P_{in} is highly dependent on the reduction factor RF. That is, for some values of RF, P_{in} may contain some points that belong to P_{on}. Hence, we might end up finding an approximated $MBC(P)$. For example, in Figure 10.2(a) we show an example of a set of points (P) to which we applied two different values of RF. $RedMBR1$ contains two points (the black vertices) that should belong to P_{on}, therefore, the calculated MBC is an approximation of the original MBC. However, $RedMBR2$ does not contain the two black vertices, hence, the algorithm finds the exact MBC. Therefore, we need to find the optimal values of RF that would produce the exact MBC.

Given P and $MBC(P)$, the largest bounding rectangle of the points in P could be the circumscribed rectangle of $MBC'(P)$ ($CirMBR$), and their smallest bounding rectangle that could fit inside $MBC(P)$ is the inscribed rectangle of $MBC(P)$ ($InsMBR$) (see Figure 10.2(b) for further details). $InsMBR$ can be considered as the largest (and hence optimal) MBR that approximates P_{in}, and the points inside $InsMBR$ (s) are a subset of P_{in} (in Figure 10.2(b), the stripped area represents s, and the gray area represents $P_{in} - s$). The smallest reduction factor RF for which $MBC(P)$ is always exact should satisfy the following relation: $RF \geq 1 - \frac{r}{D} \equiv RF \geq 1 - \frac{r}{\sqrt{2} \times r} \Rightarrow RF \geq 1 - \frac{1}{\sqrt{2}}$. In general $maxR \geq r$ (as shown in Figure 10.3), however, $MBR(P) \leq CirMBR$. Hence, by constraining RF to be $\geq 1 - \frac{1}{\sqrt{2}}$, we are guaranteeing that $RedMBR$ is always a subset of $InsMBR$. For example, in Figure 10.3 the points inside the gray area belong to $InsMBR$. However, to guarantee that we compute the exact $MBC(P)$, those points were not included inside $RedMBR$ (approximation of P_{in}).

We conducted two experiments to evaluate our proposed method over real and synthetic data. In the first experiment, we used a database of 100 real objects (contours of fish images) with an average number of points in an object equal to 100. We varied the reduction factor RF from 2% to 98% with an increment of 2. Figure 10.4(a) illustrates the results where the X-axis is percentage of reduction factor (RF), and the Y-axis is the percentage of reduction in the number of vertices and percentage of

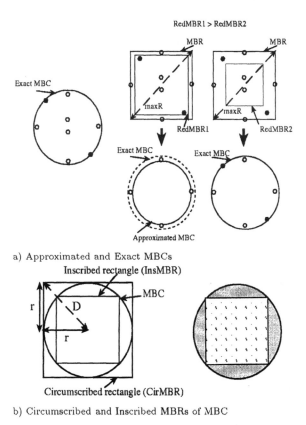

a) Approximated and Exact MBCs

b) Circumscribed and Inscribed MBRs of MBC

Figure 10.2.   MBC and its MBRs

reduction in the execution time of the optimized MBC computation algorithm as compared to the original MBC algorithm. The percentage of
reduction in the number of vertices measures the quality of our proposed
algorithm in identifying the points of an object that will not contribute in
computing $MBC(P)$. That is, it computes $\frac{P-RedMBR}{P}$. The percentage
of reduction in the execution time of MBC computation algorithm measures the time saved by not considering the points in $RedMBR$ in the
computation of its MBC. That is, $\frac{Time(MBC(P))-Time(OptimizedMBC(P))}{Time(MBC(P))}$.
From the results in Figure 10.4(a) we can conclude that our proposed algorithm reduces the execution time of $MBC(P)$ significantly (up to 90%
reduction for $RF = 4\%$). As the value of RF increases, the percentage
of reduction in the number of vertices and hence in the execution time
decreases. As a consequence, the maximum reduction in the execution

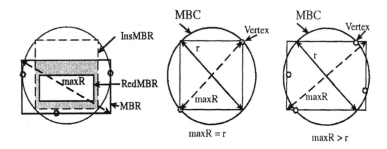

Figure 10.3. maxR

time of $MBC(P)$ for values of $RF \geq$ *optimal value of RF* was 60%. However, we were able to find the exact MBC even for cases where $RF <$ *optimal value of RF* (*i.e.*, $RF < 1 - \frac{1}{\sqrt{2}}$). The smallest value of RF without producing approximate MBCs was 4%.

In the second experiment, we used a database of 100 synthetic objects with an average number of points in an object equal to 135. The synthetic data were generated with more points inside P_{in} than the real data. We varied the reduction factor RF from 2% to 98% with an increment of 2. Figure 10.4(b) illustrates the results where the X-axis is percentage of reduction factor (RF), and the Y-axis is the percentage of reduction in the number of vertices and percentage of reduction in the execution time of MBC computation. From the results in Figure 10.4(b), we can conclude that the optimized MBC computation algorithm performed marginally better than the case where we were using real data (about 5% increase in performance). This is due to the fact that the real data had fewer points inside $InsMBR$ and hence smaller values of reduction in the number of vertices. The smallest value of RF without producing approximate MBCs was 12%. Our experimental results were consistent with our analytical observations. In all our experiments the proposed method reduced the execution time of the MBC computation algorithm. In addition, even for values of $RF < 1 - \frac{1}{\sqrt{2}}$, we still sometimes compute the exact MBC.

2. Phase Values Trends of Fourier Transform

For similarity search, a shape representation technique should be capable of supporting different types of similarity search queries such as:

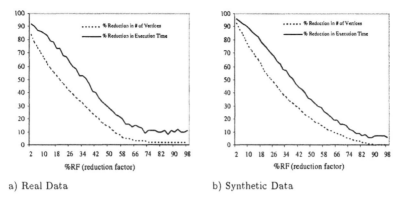

a) Real Data   b) Synthetic Data

Figure 10.4.   Performance Improvement

1) exact match, 2) exact match regardless (invariant) of size and orientation 3) exact match under specified rotation angles, scaling factors, translation vectors, or any combination of the three. The support for query types under a specified size and/or orientation is essential in some application domains.

With *MBC-based* approaches, a subset of the *MBC* features (*i.e.*, radius r, center C, and start point SP) is utilized to support match queries under a specified size and/or orientation (see [85] for further details). Our analytical studies in [84] showed that the algorithm to find similar objects in a database under a specified rotation angle incurred the highest cost $(O(N^3))$; where N is the number of vertices of an object. This is due to the fact that rotating objects would lead to different SPs, and hence resulting in various angle sequences (ASs). As a consequence, given a query object, we have to submit more queries to the database to find the candidate objects for match. To address this problem, we study the impact of using different starting points (SPs) on the phase values of the Fourier transform of a real sequence.

Consider an N-dimensional real sequence $X = (x_0, \ldots, x_{N-1})$. The Discrete Fourier transform (DFT) of X is the N-dimensional complex sequence $\hat{X} = (\hat{x}_0, \ldots, \hat{x}_{N-1})$ given by $\hat{X} = F(X)$ where

$$\hat{x}_f = \frac{1}{\sqrt{N}} \sum_{t=0}^{N-1} x_t \exp(\frac{-j2\pi f \times t}{N}) \quad ; f = 0, 1, \ldots, N-1 \qquad (10.1)$$

where j is the imaginary unit $(j = \sqrt{-1})$ of a complex number. In general, a complex number $a = \alpha + j\beta$ can be defined as the set $\| a \|$ (i.e., the magnitude of a) and $\angle a$ (i.e., the phase of a). In our discussion hereon, we assume that N is even for simplicity, although our observations extend to the case of arbitrary N. It is well known that Fast Fourier Transform (FFT) can be used to calculate the DFT coefficients in $O(N \log N)$ arithmetic operations. Some fundamental properties of the DFT are: 1) if we start with an N-dimensional nonnegative real sequence X, then $\hat{X}$ is a complex sequence with the exception of $\hat{x}_0$, which is a nonnegative real number $(\hat{x}_0 = \frac{\sum_{t=0}^{N-1} x_t}{\sqrt{N}})$, 2) the phase values for $\hat{x}_0$ and $\hat{x}_{\lceil \frac{N}{2} \rceil}$ are always equal to zero regardless of the real sequence, 3) $\hat{x}_i$ and $\hat{x}_{N-i}$ are conjugate complex numbers for $i = 1, 2, \ldots, \lceil \frac{N}{2} \rceil$, hence, $\| \hat{x}_i \| = \| \hat{x}_{N-i} \|$ (*i.e.*, their magnitudes are equal), and $\angle \hat{x}_i = -\angle \hat{x}_{N-i}$ (*i.e.*, the absolute value of their phases are equal). Figure 10.5 shows the symmetry of the magnitude and phase values of the Fourier transform of a real sequence, and 4) when applying a linear shift to a periodic sequence (or a circular shift of a sequence), we observe the circular shift property of the DFT [58] as follows: $\vec{X}[m] = \exp^{-j(\frac{2\pi m}{N})n} X[m]$ (for $0 \leq m \leq N - 1$); where $\| a \| = \sqrt{\alpha^2 + \beta^2}$ and

$$\angle a = \begin{cases} \arctan(\frac{\beta}{\alpha}) & : & \textit{if } \alpha \geq 0 \\ \arctan(\frac{\beta}{\alpha}) + \pi & : & \textit{if } \alpha < 0 \textit{ and } \beta \geq 0 \\ \arctan(\frac{\beta}{\alpha}) - \pi & : & \textit{if } \alpha < 0 \textit{ and } \beta < 0 \end{cases} \tag{10.2}$$

In this work, we investigate how to improve the response time of *MBC-based* methods for match queries under a specified rotation angle by utilizing the circular shift property of the Fourier transform of a real sequence. In addition, from our following analytical models, we will show that only one single phase value (second phase value of a sequence) is stored instead of all the phase values for different rotations/shifting to enhance the query response time of match queries under a specified rotation angle. To this end, we study the impact of using different starting points (*i.e.* rotating an object or shifting the angle sequence) on the second phase value of the discrete Fourier transform of a real sequence. If we consider an N-dimensional real sequence $X = (x_0, \ldots, x_{N-1})$, then the rotated (shifted) sequence of X is the N-dimensional sequence $\vec{X} = (x_n, \ldots, x_{N-2}, x_{N-1}, x_0, x_1, \ldots, x_{n-1})$; where

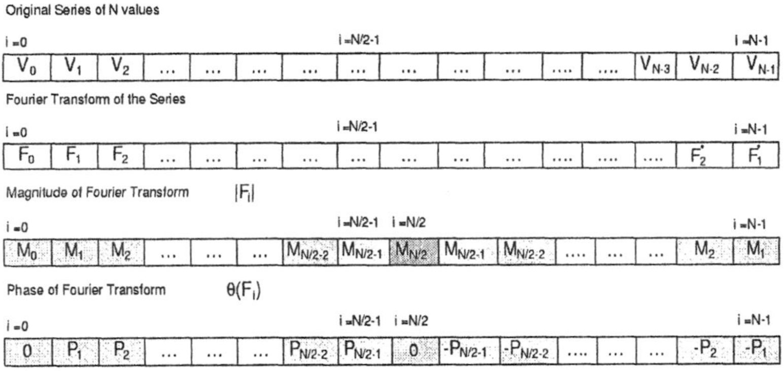

Figure 10.5.   Symmetry in Fourier Transform

n is the number of rotations. From the circular shift property of *DFT* we can conclude that the magnitude values of a Fourier transform does not change with different start points, and that the symmetry property of the phase values of the transformed sequence is still observed. However, the phase values change depending on the number of rotations. Our study shows that by applying a transformation to the Fourier components with negative phase values we can observe a new trend in the phase values of the *DFT* of a sequence. Each Fourier component is a vector in complex plane, hence, if we replace the vectors with negative phase values with vectors with the same magnitude but in the opposite direction (same effect as adding a π to the phase values) we observe the new trend. Figure 10.6 shows the phase values of a Fourier transformation of a real sequence for different number of rotations/shifting ($0 \leq number\ of\ rotations \leq N-1$) after adding π to the negative values. From Figure 10.6 we observe that after $\frac{N}{2}$ rotations of the original sequence, the phase values repeat, i.e., $\angle \hat{X}_i = \angle \hat{X}_{\frac{N}{2}+i}$, $i = 0, 1, \ldots, \frac{N}{2} - 1$; where i is the number of times the original sequence (X) is rotated. To store the phase values of the Fourier transform of a real sequence of size N for different rotation values of $0, \ldots, N-1$, a space of $\frac{N^2 - 2 \times N}{2}$ would be required. However, using our observations about the symmetry of the phase values under rotation (for rotation values of $0, \ldots, N-1$), only a space of $\frac{N^2 - 2 \times N}{4}$ is required (half the space).

In addition, from our following analytical models, we will show that only one single phase value (second phase value of a sequence) is stored

Position i =1						i =N/2-1	i =N/2		
#Rotations j =0									
0	$P_{1,2}$	$P_{1,3}$	...	...	...	$P_{1,N/2-1}$	$P_{1,N/2}$	0	...
0	$P_{2,2}$	$P_{2,3}$	...	...	...	$P_{2,N/2-1}$	$P_{2,N/2}$	0	...
...	...	...				...	...	...	
j =N/2-1 0	$P_{N/2,2}$	$P_{N/2,3}$	...	...	...	$P_{N/2,N/2-1}$	$P_{N/2,N/2}$	0	...
j =N/2 0	$P_{1,2}$	$P_{1,3}$	...	...	...	$P_{1,N/2-1}$	$P_{1,N/2}$	0	...
0	$P_{2,2}$	$P_{2,3}$	...	...	...	$P_{2,N/2-1}$	$P_{2,N/2}$	0	...
...	...	...				...	...	...	
j =N-1 0	$P_{N/2,2}$	$P_{N/2,3}$	...	...	...	$P_{N/2,N/2-1}$	$P_{N/2,N/2}$	0	...

Figure 10.6. Phase Trend with Rotation/Shifting

instead of all the phase values for different rotations/shifting to enhance the query response time of match queries under a specified rotation angle.

We define a function $\delta_{k,i,j}$ as follows:

$$\delta_{k,i,j} = \begin{cases} \angle \hat{x}_k^j - \angle \hat{x}_k^i & : \quad if \ \angle \hat{x}_k^j - \angle \hat{x}_k^i \geq 0 \\ \angle \hat{x}_k^j - \angle \hat{x}_k^i + \pi & : \quad if \ \angle \hat{x}_k^j - \angle \hat{x}_k^i < 0 \end{cases} \qquad (10.3)$$

for $k, i, j = 1, \ldots, N$; where $\angle \hat{x}_k^i$ and $\angle \hat{x}_k^j$ are the phase values of the kth component of $\hat{X}$ after $i - 1$ and $j - 1$ rotations of the real sequence X, respectively. In Figure 10.7 we show the value of the function $\delta_{k,i,j}$ for $k = 2$, $j = 1, \ldots, N$, and $i = 1, \ldots, (\frac{N}{2} + 1)$. For $i = (\frac{N}{2} + 1), \ldots, N$ the values of $\delta_{k,i,j}$ are the same as for $i = 1, \ldots, \frac{N}{2}$ but were not included in the table to save space. If we define δ as follows: given two real sequences $X1$ and $X2$ with the second phase values of their Fourier transforms $\angle \hat{X}1_1$ and $\angle \hat{X}2_1$, then:

$$\delta = \begin{cases} \frac{\angle \hat{X}1_1 - \angle \hat{X}2_1}{\frac{2 \times \pi}{N}} & : \quad if \ \angle \hat{X}1_1 - \angle \hat{X}2_1 \geq 0 \\ \frac{\angle \hat{X}1_1 - \angle \hat{X}2_1}{\frac{2 \times \pi}{N}} + \frac{N}{2} & : \quad if \ \angle \hat{X}1_1 - \angle \hat{X}2_1 < 0 \end{cases} \qquad (10.4)$$

From Figure 10.7, we can conclude the following: if we have two similar real sequences $X1$ and $X2$ (*i.e.,* the Euclidean distance between the magnitude values of their Fourier transforms ($\hat{X}1$ and $\hat{X}2$) is close to zero), then by using the phase values $\angle \hat{X}1_1$ and $\angle \hat{X}2_1$ we can tell if $X1$ and $X2$ are exactly the same or a rotated version of each other under a specific rotation value according to the following condition:

$\Delta l = (2\pi/N)$

i=1										i=N/2+1		
0	(N/2-1)Δl	(N/2-2)Δl	...	...	...	...	...	...	...	Δl	0	...
Δl	0	(N/2-1)Δl	(N/2-2)Δl	...	...	...	...	...	...	2Δl	Δl	...
2Δl	Δl	0	(N/2-1)Δl	(N/2-2)Δl	...	...	...	...	...	...	2Δl	...
...	2Δl	Δl	0	(N/2-1)Δl	(N/2-2)Δl	...	...	...	...	(N/2-2)Δl	...	...
(N/2-2)Δl	...	2Δl	Δl	0	(N/2-1)Δl	(N/2-2)Δl	...	...	...	(N/2-1)Δl	(N/2-2)Δl	...
(N/2-1)Δl	(N/2-2)Δl	...	2Δl	Δl	0	(N/2-1)Δl	(N/2-2)Δl	...	...	0	(N/2-1)Δl	...
0	(N/2-1)Δl	(N/2-2)Δl	...	2Δl	Δl	0	(N/2-1)Δl	(N/2-2)Δl	...	Δl	0	...
Δl	0	(N/2-1)Δl	(N/2-2)Δl	...	2Δl	Δl	0	(N/2-1)Δl	(N/2-2)Δl	...	Δl	...
...	Δl	0	(N/2-1)Δl	(N/2-2)Δl	...	2Δl	Δl	0	(N/2-1)Δl	(N/2-2)Δl	...	...
(N/2-2)Δl	...	Δl	0	(N/2-1)Δl	(N/2-2)Δl	...	2Δl	Δl	0	(N/2-1)Δl	(N/2-2)Δl	...
(N/2-1)Δl	(N/2-2)Δl	...	Δl	0	(N/2-1)Δl	(N/2-2)Δl	...	2Δl	Δl	0	(N/2-1)Δl	...

Figure 10.7. Phase Difference Trend

$$\theta = (2\,\pi/N)$$

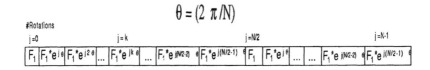

Figure 10.8. Trends in Second Phase Value

- if $\delta = 0 \longrightarrow X1$ and $X2$ are exactly the same, or rotated clockwise $\frac{N}{2}$ times

- if $\delta = n \longrightarrow$ same real sequences but shifted to the left n times, or $n + \frac{N}{2}$

where $1 \le n \le \frac{N}{2} - 1$. To generalize our observations, if $F1$ is the second Fourier coefficient of $\hat{X}$, then second Fourier coefficient of $\hat{X}$ after k shifts can be computed as $F1 \times e^{jk\theta}$ (see Figure 10.8).

Chapter 11

APPENDIX

Appendix: Cost Analysis of Index Structures
Introduction

This appendix describes the algorithm used to find the minimum bounding circle of an object and provides the cost analysis for our MBC-based methods.

1.   MBC Algorithm

A minimum bounding circle of any finite set of points ;P ; in a 2D plane is the smallest enclosing circle. We could divide the set of points of P into two sets P_{in} and P_{on} (touch points); where P_{in} is the set of all points that are contained by the MBC but are not on its boundary and P_{on} is the set of all points that contained by the MBC and are on its boundary. To compute the MBC of an object we use a simple randomized algorithm which computes the smallest enclosing disk(circle) of a set of n points in the plane in expected $O(n)$ (linear time) based on Seidels linear programming algorithm, for detail information about MBC algorithm see [97].

In [97] a lemma states that if P and R are finite point sets in the plane, P nonempty. Then, if there exists a disk containing P with R on its boundary, then the minimum bounding disk of P and R is unique.

Proposition 1.1: *The angle between any two consecutive points in a sequence of points on the MBC of a polygon (e.g. any two consecutive vertices in the set SV^i) is less than or equal to π.*

Proof: Assume that we have two consecutive points a and b, where a is before b in the sequence of touch points of MBC'. Assume also that the angle φ between them is greater than π and less than 2π . Without loss of generality , we take the example in Figure A.1-(a). There is no point of the polygon section l_3 (connecting a and b) that is on MBC' . Let C' be the center of MBC' and r' be its radius. If we move MBC' upwards until it touches a point or more on the polygon section l_3 , we will end up with a new minimum bounding circle MBC'' that encloses the same object with the same radius but different center C'' . This implies that we have two different minimum bounding circles for the same set of points (see Figure A.1-(b)). This is a contradiction , since a minimum bounding circle of any set of points should be unique (according to lemma in [97]). Then our assumption that MBC' is the minimum bounding circle was incorrect.

The second situation would be that the object has no points between a and b , then we could find a new minimum bounding circle MBC''' which encloses the objects (see Figure A.1-(c)) with a smaller radius r'' and a different center, which also contradicts our assumption. The above two cases imply that if the angle between two points on a minimum bounding circle is greater than π , then we must have at least one point between them in the sequence that is on the minimum bounding circle of the object. Thus the angle between any two points between a and b is less than π , since we are dividing an angle between π and less than 2π between two intervals or more. ∎

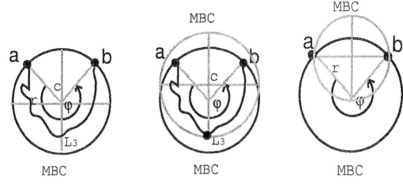

(a): Original object and its MBC

(b): MBC' enclosing the original object but with different center

(c): MBC'' enclosing the original object but with different radius

Figure A.1. Uniqueness of MBC

2.   Index Cost Analysis

This section provides the cost analysis for our methods. In [3] a computational algorithm PC is given that tests two objects O^i and O^j for similarity in $O(m^{i^8})$; where $m^i = m^j$. This complexity does not include testing for scaling-invariance nor similarity, it only tests if O^i and O^j would be similar under translation and rotation invariance. For our case, we have a reduced cost for testing for exact match between two polygons; since we get more information from the index. In computing the total cost for each technique, we consider two costs. The first is the I/O cost measured as the number of access to an index structure and the other cost would be the CPU cost measured as the number of CPU operations required to solve the problem. We also assume that the complexity of accessing the hash table is of $O(1)$. For computing the number of I/O operations assume that all objects take the same time to be retrieved from the disk. Let the total number of objects in a database equal to n and the total number of objects having the same number of vertices v equal to n_v.

- $\mathbf{I}_{\textbf{Naive}}$. $Cost_{I_{NAIVE}} = O_{hash-table} + n_v O_{PC}$. Where, $O_{hash-table}$ is the total time required to search the hash table for the objects with the same number of vertices as the query object; $O(1)$, plus the time required to retrieve those objects;$O(n_v)$. O_{PC} is the time required to compare a retrieved object with the O^q; $O(v^8)$.

- $\mathbf{I}_{\textbf{TPAS}}$. Let's assume that n_{TPAS} determines the total number of objects in the database that have the same $TPAS$ and the same number of vertices as the query objects. $Cost_{TPAS} = O_{group} + O_{R^*-treeSearch} + n_{TPAS} O_{PC-TPAS}$, where O_{group} is the time required to find the objects with the same n_{TP} and vertices as the query object using the hash tables. This cost would be of $O(1)$. $O_{R^*-treeSearch}$ is the total time required to search the index for the objects with the same $TPAS$ as O^q; $O(n_{TPAS})$, plus the time required to retrieve those objects;$O(n_{TPAS})$. $O_{PC-TPAS}$ would be $O(v)$ for **EM** queries and $O(n_{TP} * v^2)$ for **RST** queries.

- **I**_{**TPVAS**} . Suppose the total number of objects in the database that have the same VAS, the same n_{TP}, and the same number of vertices as the query objects is n_{TPVAS}. $Cost_{TPVAS} = O_{cluster} + O_{R^*-treeSearch} + n_{TPVAS}O_{PC-TPVAS}$; where, O_{group} is the time required to find the objects with same n_{TP} as the query object using the hash table; $O(1)$. $O_{R^*-treeSearch}$ is the total time required to search the index for the objects with the same VAS as O^q; $O(n_{TPVAS})$, plus the time required to retrieve those objects; $O(n_{TPVAS})$. $O_{PC-TPVAS}$ would be $O(v)$ for **EM** queries and $O(v^3)$ for **RST** queries.

- **I**_{**VAS**} . Suppose that the total number of objects in the database that have the same VAS, and the same number of vertices as the query objects equals to n_{VAS}. $Cost_{VAS} = O_{R^*-treeSearch} + n_{VAS}O_{PC-VAS}$, where, $O_{R^*-treeSearch}$ is the total time required to search the index for the objects with the same VAS as O^q; $O(n_{VAS})$, plus the time required to retrieve those objects; $O(n_{VAS})$. O_{PC-VAS} would be $O(v)$ for **EM** queries, and $O(v^3)$ for both **RST** and **SIM** queries.

Appendix: Spatial Relations with MBR

Spatial Relations Using Minimum Bounding Rectangles

Introduction

This appendix describes the primitive topological and direction relation sets as defined in [63, 62, 92, 64, 25]. We start by defining the *primitive topological relations* as defined by the 9-*intersection* model for objects represented by their *MBR*. Then we define the two topological relation sets *mt1* and *mt2* as defined in [64]. Finally, we present a table that presents the relations that should be satisfied in order to propagate into intermediate nodes in a tree structure and a table that shows the empty results queries.

1.   Topological Relations Using MBRs

We first start by showing all the possible topological relations between *MBRs* as defined by the 9-*intersection* model. These relations are illustrated in Figure B.1. The corresponding topological relations for objects approximated by their *MBC* are shown in Figure B.2.

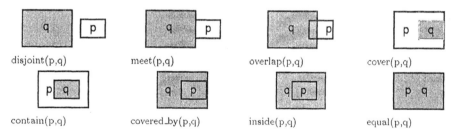

Figure B.1.   Possible topological relations between MBRs

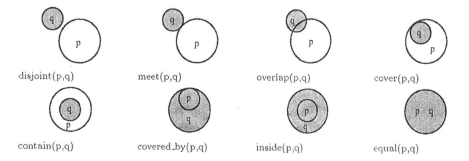

Figure B.2.   Possible topological relations between MBCs

Table B.1.   Relations for the intermediate nodes

Relation be-tween $MBCs$	Relations between intermediate node P (that may enclose MBC $p\prime$) and reference MBC
$equal(p\prime, q\prime)$	$equal(P, q\prime) \lor cover(P, q\prime) \lor contain(P, q\prime)$
$contain(p\prime, q\prime)$	$contain(P, q\prime)$
$inside(p\prime, q\prime)$	$overlap(P, q\prime) \lor equal(P, q\prime) \lor inside(P, q\prime)$ $cover(P, q\prime) \lor covered\_by(P, q\prime) \lor contain(P, q\prime)$
$cover(p\prime, q\prime)$	$cover(P, q\prime) \lor contain(P, q\prime)$
$covered\_by(p\prime, q\prime)$	$overlap(P, q\prime) \lor equal(P, q\prime) \lor cover(P, q\prime)$ $covered\_by(P, q\prime) \lor contain(P, q\prime)$
$disjoint(p\prime, q\prime)$	$overlap(P, q\prime) \lor meet(P, q\prime) \lor cover(P, q\prime)$ $contain(P, q\prime) \lor disjoint(P, q\prime)$
$meet(p\prime, q\prime)$	$contain(P, q\prime) \lor cover(P, q\prime) \lor meet(P, q\prime)$ $overlap(P, q\prime)$
$overlap(p\prime, q\prime)$	$contain(P, q\prime) \lor cover(P, q\prime) \lor overlap(P, q\prime)$

Topological relation set $mt1$ consists of the relations *disjoint* and *not-disjoint*. This set is used if the only topological relation of interest is to check if two objects share some common points or not. A second set of topological relations is named $mt2$ [64]. This set consists of the topological relations described in Figure B.1: *disjoint*, *meet*, *overlap*, *cover*, *contain*, *covered_by*, *inside*, and *equal*.

Table B.1 presents the relations that may be satisfied between an intermediate node P and the $q\prime$ of the *reference* object, so that the node be selected for propagation in the tree structure as in [64].

Tables B.2 and B.3, illustrate the relations between *reference* object and *primary* objects for which an empty result is returned without running the query as in [64]. When a query involving two *reference* objects $q1$ and $q2$ is given, if the topological relation between the *reference* objects exists in Tables B.2 and B.3, the output of the query is empty. For the above query, in addition to *meet* , if $q1$ and $q2$ are related by *equal, contain, disjoint* or *covered_by*, the result is also empty. Each entry at row $ri(p,q1)$ and column $rj(p,q2)$ (where ri and rj are relations of $mt2$) is the composition of the relations $ri(p,q1)$ and $rj(p,q2)$ with respect to $mt2$.

2.   Direction Relations Using MBRs

This section describes two sets of direction relations $d1$ and $d2$ as defined in [63]. The set $d1$ is the set of primitive direction relation that is constructed based on *projection-based* method. It contains nine primitive relations defined as follows:

- $Restricted\text{-}North(p_i, q_j) \equiv X(p_i) = X(q_j) \land Y(p_i) > Y(q_j)$
- $North\text{-}East(p_i, q_j) \equiv X(p_i) > X(q_j) \land Y(p_i) > Y(q_j)$
- $North\text{-}West(p_i, q_j) \equiv X(p_i) < X(q_j) \land Y(p_i) > Y(q_j)$

Table B.2.   MBC relations and empty results queries

	d(p,q2)	m(p,q2)	e(p,q2)	i(p,q2)	cb(p,q2)	ct(p,q2)	cv(p,q2)	o(p,q2)
d(p,q1)	—	e V ct V cv	m V e V i V cb V ct V cv V o	e V ct V cv	e V ct V cv	m V e V i V cb V ct V cv V o	m V e V i V cb V ct V cv V o	e V ct V cv
m(p,q1)	e V i V cb	i V ct	d V e V i V cb V ct V cv V o	d V m V e V ct V cv	d V e V ct V cv	m V e V i V cb V ct V cv V o	e V i V cb V ct V cv V o	e V ct V cv
e(p,q1)	m V e V i V cb V ct V cv V o	d V e V i V cb V ct V cv V o	d V m V i V cb V ct V cv V o	d V m V e V cb V ct V cv V o	d V m V e V i V ct V cv V o	d V m V e V i V cb V cv V o	d V m V e V i V cb V ct	d V m V e V i V cb V ct V cv
i(p,q1)	e V i V cb	d V m V e V i V cb	d V m V e V i V cb V cv V o	d V m	d V m V e V i V cb V o	d V m V e V i V cb V cv V o	d V m V e V i V cb V cv	d V m V e V i V cb

Where d: *disjoint*, m: *meet*, e: *equal*, i: *inside*, cb: *covered_by*, ct: *contain*, cv: *cover*, and o: *overlap*

Table B.3.   Cont. MBC relations and empty results queries

	d(p,q2)	m(p,q2)	e(p,q2)	i(p,q2)	cb(p,q2)	ct(p,q2)	cv(p,q2)	o(p,q2)
cb(p,q1)	e V i V cb	d V e V i V cb	d V m V e V i V cb V ct V o	d V m V e V ct V cv	d V m V i V ct	d V m V e V i V cb V cv V o	d V m V e V i V cb V o	d V m V e V i V cb
ct(p,q1)	m V e V i V cb V ct V cv V o	m V e V i V cb V ct V cv V o	d V m V e cb V ct V cv V o	d V m V e V cb V ct V cv V o	d V m V e V cb V ct V cv V o	—	e V ct V cv	e V ct V cv
cv(p,q1)	m V e V i V cb V ct V cv V o	e V i V cb V ct V cv V o	d V m V e V i V ct V cv V o	d V m V e V cb V ct V cv V o	d V m V e V ct V cv V o	e V i V cb	i V ct	e V ct V cv
o(p,q1)	e V i V cb	e V i V cb	d V m V e V i V cb V ct V cv	d V m V e V ct V cv	d V m V e V ct V cv	e V i V cb	e V i V cb	—

Where d: *disjoint*, m: *meet*, e: *equal*, i: *inside*, cb: *covered_by*, ct: *contain*, cv: *cover*, and o: *overlap*

- $Restricted\text{-}South(p_i, q_j) \equiv X(p_i) = X(q_j) \wedge Y(p_i) < Y(q_j)$
- $South\text{-}East(p_i, q_j) \equiv X(p_i) > X(q_j) \wedge Y(p_i) < Y(q_j)$
- $South\text{-}West(p_i, q_j) \equiv X(p_i) < X(q_j) \wedge Y(p_i) < Y(q_j)$
- $Restricted\text{-}East(p_i, q_j) \equiv X(p_i) > X(q_j) \wedge Y(p_i) = Y(q_j)$
- $Restricted\text{-}West(p_i, q_j) \equiv X(p_i) < X(q_j) \wedge Y(p_i) = Y(q_j)$
- $Same\text{-}Position(p_i, q_j) \equiv X(p_i) = X(q_j) \wedge Y(p_i) = Y(q_j)$

where X and Y are functions that return the x and y coordinates of a point.

The set $d2$ of directional relations of contain more general relations generated from disjunction of relations of set $d1$. The relations of set $d2$ were defined as follows:

- $North(p_i, q_j) \equiv North\text{-}West(p_i, q_j) \wedge Restricted\text{-}North(p_i, q_j) \wedge North\text{-}East(p_i, q_j)$

- $East(p_i, q_j) \equiv North\text{-}East(p_i, q_j) \wedge Restricted\text{-}East(p_i, q_j) \wedge South\text{-}East(p_i, q_j)$

- $South(p_i, q_j) \equiv South\text{-}West(p_i, q_j) \wedge Restricted\text{-}South(p_i, q_j) \wedge South\text{-}East(p_i, q_j)$

- $West(p_i, q_j) \equiv North\text{-}West(p_i, q_j) \wedge Restricted\text{-}West(p_i, q_j) \wedge South\text{-}West(p_i, q_j)$

- $Same\text{-}Level(p_i, q_j) \equiv Restricted\text{-}West(p_i, q_j) \wedge Same\text{-}Position(p_i, q_j) \wedge Restricted\text{-}East(p_i, q_j)$

- $Same\text{-}Width(p_i, q_j) \equiv Restricted\text{-}North(p_i, q_j) \wedge Same\text{-}Position(p_i, q_j) \wedge Restricted\text{-}South(p_i, q_j)$

Using both sets $d1$ and $d2$ of directional relations between points, the directional relationships between objects could be defined as follows:

- $Strong\text{-}North(p, q) \equiv \forall p_i \, \forall q_j \, North(p_i, q_j)$

- $Weak\text{-}North(p, q) \equiv \exists p_i \, \forall q_j \, North(p_i, q_j) \wedge \forall p_i \, \exists q_j \, North(p_i, q_j) \wedge \exists p_i \, \exists q_j \, South(p_i, q_j)$

- $Strong\text{-}Bounded\text{-}North(p, q) \equiv \forall p_i \, \forall q_j \, North(p_i, q_j) \wedge \forall p_i \, \exists q_j \, North\text{-}East(p_i, q_j) \wedge \forall p_i \, \exists q_j \, North\text{-}West(p_i, q_j)$

- $Weak\text{-}Bounded\text{-}North(p, q) \equiv \exists p_i \, \forall q_j \, North(p_i, q_j) \wedge \exists p_i \, \exists q_j \, South(p_i, q_j) \wedge \forall p_i \, \exists q_j \, North\text{-}East(p_i, q_j) \wedge \forall p_i \, \exists q_j \, North\text{-}West(p_i, q_j)$

- $Strong\text{-}North\text{-}East(p, q) \equiv \forall p_i \, \forall q_j \, North\text{-}East(p_i, q_j)$

- $Weak\text{-}North\text{-}East(p, q) \equiv \exists p_i \, \forall q_j \, North\text{-}East(p_i, q_j) \wedge \exists p_i \, \exists q_j \, South(p_i, q_j) \wedge \forall p_i \, \exists q_j \, North\text{-}East(p_i, q_j)$

- $Just\text{-}North(p, q) \equiv \forall p_i \, \forall q_j \, (North(p_i, q_j) \wedge Same\text{-}Level(p_i, q_j)) \wedge \exists p_i \, \exists q_j \, Same\text{-}Level(p_i, q_j) \wedge \exists p_i \, \exists q_j \, North(p_i, q_j)$

- $North(p, q) \equiv \exists p_i \, \forall q_j \, North(p_i, q_j) \wedge \forall p_i \, \exists q_j \, North(p_i, q_j)$

Appendix: Computation and Storage Cost Analysis

Computation and Storage Cost Analysis For Alternative Shape Representation Techniques

Introduction

This appendix provides cost analysis for the different methods and compares their efficiency in terms of computation and storage requirements.

1.　　Grid Based Method

For the GB method, we assume that: the grid cell size $gn X gn$, the standardized major axis size mj, total number of pixels of the grid $px = mj^2$, number of coordinates of object N, and binary sequence size $SS = (mj/gn)^2/8$ bytes. Then the following storage is required for the shape signatures:

- 8 bytes to store the eccentricity of each shape (one real number).

- $SS = ((mj/gn)^2)/8$ *bytes* to store one binary sequence.

- $2*n*SS+8*n$ *bytes* to store n shape signatures (assuming at least 2 sequences per object).

- A temporary storage of $px/8$ bytes per object.

To compute the shape signature for the query object and to compute the similarity between the query object and the objects in the database the following major operations are required :

- To find major axis $O(N^2)$

- To find minor axis $O(N)$

- To rotate and scale $O(N)$

- To check if a point is inside a polygon $O(N)$

- To generate a binary number we need to check all the grid cells/ pixels to see if they are inside the shape $O(px * N)$. Usually $\sqrt{px} \geq N$, therefore $O(px * N) \approx O(N^3)$.

- For each similarity calculation we need: *exclusive OR* between the query binary sequence and the stored-shape binary sequence, and count the number of ones in the result. Hence, similarity calculation takes around $8 * SS$ bits XOR operations and $8 * SS$ bits additions.

2.　　Fourier Descriptors Method

For the FD method, we assume that: number of radii equals to r, number of Fourier coefficients is fn, number of coordinates of an object N. Then the following storage is required for the shape signatures:

- To store one shape signature: $8 * fn$ *bytes*.

- To store n shape signatures: $8 * n * fn$ *bytes*.

To compute the shape signature for the query object and to compute the similarity between the query object and the objects in the database the following major operations are required :

- To find centroid $O(NlogN)$ (we compute the Delaunay triangulation to this end).

- To find all radii and to compute FD coefficients $O(r^2)$.

- To generate shape signature $O(r)$ (required for normalization step).

- For each similarity calculation we need: fn real-number subtractions, fn real-number multiplications, $fn - 1$ real-number additions.

3.   Delaunay Triangulation Method

For the DT method, we assume that: number of bins nb, and number of coordinates of object N. Then the following storage is required for the shape signatures:

- To store one shape signature: $4 * nb$ *bytes*.

- To store n shape signatures: $4 * n * nb$ *bytes*.

- Temporary storage: $3 * N$ (per object).

To compute the shape signature for the query object and to compute the similarity between the query object and the objects in the database the following major operations are required :

- To compute the Delaunay triangulation of a shape: $O(NlogN)$.

- To generate shape signature: $O(N)$ (required to find all angles).

- For each similarity calculation we need: nb integer-number subtractions, nb integer-number multiplications, $nb - 1$ integer-number additions.

4.   MBC-TPVAS Method

For the MBC-$TPVAS$ method, we assume that: number of Fourier coefficients fn, and number of coordinates of an object N. Then the following storage is required for the shape signatures:

- To store number of touch points 1 byte.

- To store one shape signature : $8 * fn$ *bytes*.

- To store n objects: $8 * n * fn$ *bytes*.

To compute the shape signature for the query object and to compute the similarity between the query object and the objects in the database the following major operations are required :

- To find MBC $O(N)$.

- To compute angle sequence and find all DFT coefficients of an angle sequence $O(N)$.

- For each similarity calculation we need: fn real-number subtractions, fn real-number multiplications, $fn - 1$ real-number additions.

Chapter 12

BIBLIOGRAPHY
References

[1] R. Agrawal, C. Faloutsos, and A. Swami Efficient Similarity Search In Sequence Databases *FODO*,1993.

[2] R. Agrawal, K. Lin, H. Sawhney, and K. Shim Fast Similarity Search in the Presence of Noise, Scaling, and Translation in Time-Series Databases *Proceedings of the 21st VLDB Conference Zurich, Switzerland*, 1995.

[3] H. Alt, Blömer J. Resemblance and Symmetries of Geometric Patterns *Data Structures and Efficient Algorithms, in: LNCS*, Vol. 594, pp.1-24, Springer 1992.

[4] G.N. Bebis, and G.M. Papadourakis Object recognition using invariant object boundary representations and neural network models *Pattern Recognition*, Vol. 25, pp. 25-44, 1992.

[5] R. Beckmann and H.P. Kriegel The R^*-tree: An Efficient and Robust Access Method for Points and Rectangles *Proceedings ACM SIGMOD International Conference on Management of Data, Atlantic City, NJ*, pp. 322-331, 1990

[6] J.L. Bentley, and J.H. Friedman Data Structures for Range Searching. *ACM Computing Surveys*, 11(4), p. 397-409, December 1979.

[7] S. Berchtold, D. Keim, and H.P. Kriegel The $X-tree$: An Index Structure for High-Dimensional Data *Proceedings of the 22nd VLDB Conference Mumbai, India*, 1996.

[8] S. Berchtold, and H.P. Kriegel S3: Similarity Search in CAD Database Systems *SIGMOD*, 1997.

[9] S. Berchtold, D. Keim, and H.P. Kriegel Using Extended Feature Objects for Partial Similarity retrieval *VLDB*,1997.

[10] S. Berchtold, and D. Keim Section Coding; A Similarity Search Technique for the Car Manufacturing Industry *IDAT*, 1998.

[11] T. Bozkaya, and M. Ozsoyoglu Distance-Based Indexing for High-Dimensional Metric Spaces. *Proceedings of SIGMOD International Conference on Management of Data*, p. 357-368, 1997.

[12] T. Brinkhoff, H.P. Kriegel, and R. Schneider Comparison of Approximations of Complex Objects Used for Approximation-based Query Processing in Spatial Database Systems *In the Proceedings of the 9th International Conference on Data Engineering, ICDE*, 1993.

[13] P. Bruce Berra, F. Golshani, R. Mehrotra, and O. R. Sheng Guest Editors' Introduction Multimedia Information Systems *IEEE Transactions on Knowledge and data Engineering*, Vol 5, No. 4, 1993.

[14] A. Califano, and R. Mohan Multidimensional Indexing for Recognizing Visual Shapes *IEEE Transactions on Pattern Analysis and Machine Intelligence* Vol. 16, NO. 4, April 1994.

[15] C. Chung, S. Lee, S. Chun, D. Kim, and J. Lee Similarity Search for Multidimensional Data Sequences *In the Proceedings of the 16th International Conference on Data Engineering (ICDE)*, San Diego, CA, USA, February 29 - March 3, 2000.

[16] P. Ciaccia, M. Patella, and P. Zezula $M-Tree$: An Efficient Access Method for Similarity Search in Metric Spaces. *Proceedings of Very Large Data Bases Conference*, 1997.

[17] J.P. Eakins Retrieval of trade mark images by shape feature *Proceedings First International Conference on Electronic Library and Visual Information System Research, de Montfort University*, pp. 101-109, 1994.

[18] J.P. Eakins , K. Sheilds and J.M. Boardman ARTISAN– a shape retrieval system based on boundary family indexing *Storage and Retrieval for Image and Video Databases IV, (Sethi, I K and Jain, RC, eds), Proc SPIE 2670*, pp. 17-28, 1996.

[19] M.J. Egenhofer Reasoning about Binary Topological Relations. *In the Proceedings of the Second Symposium on the Design and Implementation of Large Spatial Databases, Springer-Verlag LNCS* 1991.

[20] M.J. Egenhofer On the Robustness of Qualitative Distance- and Direction-Reasoning *In the Proceedings of Auto-Carto 12, in Charlotte, North Carolina*, pp. 301-310, 1995.

[21] M.J. Egenhofer The Direction-Relation Matrix: A Representation for Direction Relations between Extended Spatial Objects *http://www.spatial.maine.edu/max/max.html* 1997.

[22] C. Faloutsos, and S. Roseman Fractals for Secondary Key Retrieval. *Technical Report UMIACS-TR-89-47, CS-TR-2242*, University of Maryland, College Park, Maryland, May 1989.

[23] C. Faloutsos, M. Ranganathan, and Y. Manolopoulos Fast Subsequence Matching in Time-Series Databases *SIGMOD*,1994.

[24] A.U. Frank Qualitative Spatial Reasoning with Cardinal Directions *Proceedings of the Seventh Austrian Conference on Artificial Intelligence, Wien, Springer*, Berlin, pp. 157-167, 1991.

[25] A.U. Frank Qualitative Spatial Reasoning about Distances and Directions in Geographic Space *Journal of Visual Languages and Computing,3* pp. 343-371, 1992.

[26] M. Freeston The BANG file: A new kind of grid file. *Proceedings of ACM SIGMOD International Conference on Management of Data,* San Francisco, CA, p. 260-269, 1987.

[27] C. Freksa Using Orientation Information for Qualitative Spatial Reasoning *In A.U. Frank, I. Campari, U. Formentini (eds.) Theories and Methods of Spatio-Temporal Reasoning in Geographic Space, LNCS 639, Springer-Verlag* Berlin, 1992.

[28] J. Gary, and R. Mehrotra Feature-Based Retrieval of Similar Shapes *International Conference on Data Engineering* 1993.

[29] J. Gary, and R. Mehrotra Similar-Shape Retrieval In Shape Data Management *IEEE, Computer* September 1995.

[30] S. Ghandeharizadeh Stream-Based Versus Structured Video Objects: Issues, Solutions, and Challenges *In S. Jajodia and V. Subrahmanian, eds, Multimedia DB Systems: Issues and Res. Direct., Springer-Verlag,* 1995.

[31] R.C. Gonzalez, and P. Wintz Digital Image Processing 2nd edition *Addison-Wesley,* Reading, Mass. 1987.

[32] G.H. Granlund Fourier preprocessing for hand print character recognition *IEEE Transactions on Computers,* C-21, pp. 195-201, Feb. 1972.

[33] D. Greene An Implementation and Performance Analysis of Spatial Data Access Methods *In the Proceedings of the 5th International Conference on Data Engineering, ICDE,* 1989.

[34] W. Grosky, P. Neo, and R. Mehrotra A Pictorial Index Mechanism fir Model-Based Matching *International Conference on Data Engineering,* 1989.

[35] W. Grosky, and R. Mehrotra Index-Based Object Recognition in Pictorial Data Management *Computer Vision, Graphics, and Image Processing* Vol. 52,p.416-436, 1990.

[36] L. Guibas and J. Stolfi Primitives for the Manipulation of General Subdivisions and the Computation of Voronoi Diagrams *ACM Transactions on Graphics*, 4:74-123, April, 1986.

[37] O. Gunther The *cell tree*: an index for geometric data. *Memorandum No. UCB/ERL M86/98* , University of California, Berkeley, December 1986.

[38] L. Guojun An approach to image retrieval based on shape *Journal of Information Science*, 23 (2), pp. 119-127, 1997.

[39] A. Guttman $R-trees$: A Dynamic Index Structure for Spatial Searching *Proceedings of ACM SIGMOD International Conference on Management of Data*, pp. 47-57, 1984.

[40] R.H. Guting An Introduction to Spatial Database Systems *Invited Contribution to a Special Issue on Spatial Database Systems of the VLDB Journal*, Vol. 3, No. 4, October 1994.

[41] Pitas, Ioannis Digital Image Processing Algorithms *Prentice Hall*, Englewood Cliffs, N.J. 1993.

[42] Jagadish H. V. A Retrieval Technique for Similarity Shapes *Proceedings of ACM SIGMOD International Conference on Management of Data*, pp. 208-217, 1991.

[43] N. Katayama, and S. Satoh The $SR-Tree$: An Index Structure for High-Dimensional Nearest Neighbor Queries. *Proceedings of SIGMOD International Conference on Management of Data*, p. 369-380, 1997.

[44] H. Kauppinen, T. Seppanen, M. Pietikainen An experimental comparison of autoregressive and Fourier-based descriptors in 2D shape classification *IEEE Transaction on Pattern Analysis and Machine Intelligence*, 17(2):201-207, 1995.

[45] W. Kim, and R.H. Park Contour coding based on the decomposition of line segments *Pattern Recognition Letters*, 11, 1999.

[46] F. Korn, N. Sidiropoulos, C. Faloutsos, E. Siegel, and Z. Protopapas Fast Nearest Neighbor Search in Medical Image Databases *Proceedings of 22nd VLDB Conference*, pp.215-226, Mumbai, India, 1996.

[47] R. Kurniawati, J.S. Jin, and J.A. Shepherd The SS^+-tree: An improved index structure for similarity searches in a high-dimensional

feature space. *Proceedings of International Conference on storage and retrieval for image and video databases (SPIE)*, 1997.

[48] C.S. Lin and C.L. Hwang New forms of shape invariants from elliptic Fourier descriptors *Pattern Recognition*, 20(5), pp. 535-545, 1987.

[49] D.B. Lomet, and B. Salzberg The $hb-tree$: a multi-attribute indexing method with good guaranteed performance. *Proceedings of ACM TODS*, 15(4), p. 625-658, December 1990.

[50] G. Lu, and A. Sajjanhar Region-based shape representation and similarity measure suitable for content-based image retrieval *Multimedia Systems 7*, Springer-Verlag, pp. 165-174, 1999(2).

[51] N. Megiddo Linear-Time Algorithms for Linear Programming in R^3 and Related Problems *SIAM Journal of Computation*, 12, 108-116, 1984.

[52] R. Mehrotra, and J.E. Gary Image retrieval using color and shape *Second Asian Conference on Computer Vision* , 5-8 December, Singapore. Springer, Berlin, pp. 529-533, 1995.

[53] B.M. Mehtre, M.S. Kankanhalli, W.F. Lee Shape Measures for Content Based Image Retrieval: A Comparison *Information Processing and Management*, Vol.33, No.3, pp. 319-337, 1997.

[54] F. Mokhtarian, S. Abbasi, and J. Kitter Efficient and Robust Retrieval by Shape Content through Curvature Scale Space *Proceedings of International Workshop on Image Database and Multimedia Search*, pp. 35-42, Amsterdam, Netherlands, 1996.

[55] W. Niblak, R. Barder, W. Equitz, M. Flickner, E. Glasman, D. Petkovic, P. Yanker, C. Faloutsos, and G. Yaubin QBIC Project: Querying images by content using color, texture, and shape. *Proceedings of SPIE Storage and Retrieval for Image and Video Databases*, vol. 1908, p. 173-181, 1993.

[56] J. Nievergelt, H. Hinterberger, and K.C. Sevcik The Grid File: An Adaptable Symmetric Multikey File Structure. *ACM Transaction on Database Systems*, 9(1), 1984.

[57] P.V. Oösterom, and E. Claassen Orientation Insensitive Indexing Methods for Geometric Objects *4th International Symposium on Spatial Data Handling, Zurich, Switzerland* p.1016-1029, 1990.

[58] A. V. Oppenheim and R.W. Schafer Digital Signal Processing *Prentice Hall*, Englewood Cliffs, N.J., 1975.

[59] J.A. Orestein Spatial Query Processing in an Object Oriented Database System. *Proceedings of ACM SIGMOD Conference on the Management of Data*, p. 326-336, Washington, U.S.A., May 1986.

[60] M. Otterman Approximate Matching with High Dimensionality *R − trees M.Sc. scholarly paper, Dept. of Computer Science, Univ, of Maryland, College Park, MD*, 1992.

[61] D. Papadias, and T. Sellis The Semantics of Relations in 2D Space Using Representative Points: Spatial Indexes *In Frank, A.U., Campari, I. (eds.) Proceedings of the European Conference on Spatial Information Theory, COSIT* Springer Verlag, 1993.

[62] D. Papadias, and Y. Theodoridis Spatial Relations, Minimum Bounding Rectangles, and Spatial Data Structures *Technical Report, KDBSLAB-TR-94-06, National Technical University of Athen, Greece*, 1994.

[63] D. Papadias, Y. Theodoridis, and T. Sellis The Retrieval of Direction Relations using *R − trees In the Proceedings of the 5th International Conference on Databases and Expert Systems Applications, DEXA* Springer Verlag, LNCS, 1994.

[64] D. Papadias, Y. Theodoridis, T. Sellis, and M.J. Egenhofer Topological Relations in the World of Minimum Bounding Rectangles: A study with *R − trees Proceedings of ACM SIGMOD International Conference on Management of Data*, 1995.

[65] C.H. Papadimitriou, D. Suciu, and V. Vianu Topological Queries in Spatial Databases *ACM PODS, Montreal Quebec, Canada*, 1996.

[66] D. Pequet, and Z. Ci-Xiang An Algorithm to Determine the Directional Relationship between Arbitrarily Shaped Polygons in the Plane *Pattern Recognition*, Vol. 20 , No. 1, pp. 65-74

[67] E. Persoon and K.S. Fu Shape discrimination using Fourier descriptors *IEEE Transactions on Systems, Man and Cybernetics*, 7, pp. 170-179, 1977.

[68] C.W. Richard Jr. and H. Hemami Identification of three--dimensional objects using Fourier descriptors of the boundary curve *IEEE Transactions on Systems, Man and Cybernetics*, SMC-4, pp. 371-378, July 1974.

[69] Robinson, J.T. *K − D − B tree*: A Search Structure for Large Multidimensional Dynamic Indices. Proceedings of ACM SIGMOD Conference on the Management of Data, 1981.

[70] M. Safar, and C. Shahabi 2D Topological and Direction Relations in the World of Minimum Bounding Circles *In the Proceedings of IEEE 1999 International Database Engineering and Applications Symposium (IDEAS)*, pp. 239-247, Montreal, Canada, August 2-4, 1999.

[71] M. Safar, Shahabi C., and Sun X. Image Retrieval By Shape: A Comparative Study *In the Proceedings of IEEE International Conference on Multimedia and Exposition (ICME)*, New York, U.S.A., July 30 - August 2, 2000.

[72] M. Safar, Shahabi C., and Tan C.H. Resiliency and Robustness of Alternative Shape-Based Image Retrieval Techniques *In the Proceedings of IEEE 2000 International Database Engineering and Applications Symposium (IDEAS)*, Japan, 2000.

[73] M. Safar, Shahabi C. A Framework To Evaluate The Effectiveness Of Shape Representation Techniques *Journal of Applied Systems Studies (JASS), special issue on "Distributed Multimedia Systems and Applications"*, 2001.

[74] M. Safar, Shahabi C. Two Optimization Techniques to Improve the Performance of MBC-based Shape Retrieval *In the Sixth International Workshop on Multimedia Information Systems (MIS)*, 2000.

[75] A. Sajjanhar, G. Lu and J. Wright An experimental study of moment invariants and Fourier descriptors for shape based image retrieval *Proceedings of the Second Australia Document Computing Symposium*, Melbourne, Australia, pp. 46-54, April 5 1997.

[76] A. Sajjanhar and G. Lu Indexing 2D non-occluded shape for similarity retrieval *SPIE Conference on Applications of Digital Image Processing XX, Proceedings*, Vol. 3164, San Diego, USA, pp.188-197, 30 July -1 August 1997.

[77] A. Sajjanhar, and G. Lu A Grid Based Shape Indexing and Retrieval Method *Special issue of Australian Computer Journal on Multimedia Storage and Archiving Systems*, Vol. 29, No.4, pp. 131-140, November 1997.

[78] A. Sajjanhar, and G. Lu A Comparison of Techniques for Shape Retrieval *International Conference on Computational Intelligence and Multimedia Applications*, Monash University, Gippsland Campus, pp.854-859, 9-11 Feb. 1998.

[79] H. Samet The Design and Analysis of Spatial Data Structures. *Addision-Wesley*, 1989.

[80] H. Samet Spatial Data Structures *In Modern Database Systems: The Object Model, Interoperability, and Beyond, W. Kim, e.d., Addison Wesley/ACM Press* pp. 361-385, 1995.

[81] B. Scassellatie, S. Alexopoulos, and M. Flickner Retrieving images by 2D shape: A comparison of computation methods with human perceptual judgments *SPIE Conference on Storage and Retrieval for Image and Video Databases II*, San Jose, CA, USA. SPIE Proceedings Vol. 2185, pp. 2-14, February 6-10, 1994.

[82] B. Seeger, and H.P. Kriegel The *Buddy Tree*: An Efficient and Robust Access Method for Spatial Database Systems. *Proceedings of 16th International Conference on Very Large Databases*, Brisbane, Australia, p. 590-601,1990.

[83] T. Sellis, N. Roussopoulos, and C. Faloutsos The R^+ *Tree*: A Dynamic Index for Multidimensional Objects. *Proceedings of 13th International Conference on Very Large Databases*, Brighton, U.K., p. 507-518, September, 1987.

[84] C. Shahabi, M. Safar, and A. Hezhi Multiple Index Structures for Efficient Retrieval of 2D Objects *In the Proceeding of IEEE 19th International Conference on Data Engineering (ICDE)*, Sydney, Australia, March 23-26, 1999.

[85] C. Shahabi, M. Safar Efficient Retrieval and Spatial Querying of 2D Objects *In the Proceedings of IEEE International Conference on Multimedia Computing and Systems (ICMCS)*, pp.611-617, June 7-11, Florence, Italy, 1999.

[86] C. Shahabi, M. Safar, and X. Sun An Experimental Study of Alternative Shape-Based Image Retrieval Techniques *Submitted to ACM Journal on Multimedia Systems*, 2000.

[87] K. Shim, R. Srikant, and R. Agrawal The ϵ-$K - D - B$ *tree*: A Fast index Structure for High-dimensional Similarity Joins. *Proceedings of the 13th International Conference on data engineering*. Birmingham, U.K., April, 1997.

[88] A.W.M. Smeulders, M. Worring, S. Santini, A. Gupta, and R. Jain Content-Based Image Retrieval at the End of the Early Years. *IEEE Transactions on Pattern Analysis and Machine Intelligence*, vol. 22, no. 12, December 2000.

[89] C.W. Sul, K.C. Lee, and K. Wohn Virtual Stage: A Location-Based Karoke System *IEEE Multimedia*, pp. 42-52, 1998.

[90] Y. Tao, and W.I. Grosky Delaunay triangulation for image object indexing: a novel method for shape representation *Proceedings of the Seventh SPIE Symposium on Storage and Retrieval for Image and Video Databases*, San Jose, California, pp.631-642, January 1999.

[91] Y. Tao, and W.I. Grosky Object-Based image retrieval using point feature maps *Proceedings of the International Conference on Database Semantics (DS-8)*, Rotorua, New Zealand, pp. 59-73, January 1999.

[92] Y. Theodoridis, D. Papadias, and E. Stefanakis Supporting Direction Relations in Spatial Database Systems *Technical Report KDBSLAB-TR-95-02, National Technical university of Athens, Greece*, 1995.

[93] Y. Theodoridis, and T. Sellis On the Performance Analysis of Multi-dimensional $R - tree - based$ Data Structures *Technical Report KDBSLAB-TR-95-03, National Technical university of Athens, Greece*, 1995.

[94] A. Thomasian, V. Castello, and C.S. Li Clustering and Singular Value Decomposition for Approximate Indexing in High Dimensional Spaces. *Proceedings of the ACM CIKM International Conference on Information and Knowledge Management*, Bethesda, Maryland, USA, November 3-7, 1998.

[95] T. Wallace and P.A. Wintz Fourier Descriptors for Extraction of Shape Information *Final Report of Research for the Period Nov. 1, 1975 - Oct. 31, 1976.*, Contract No. F 30602-75-C-0150.

[96] T.P. Wallace, and P.A. Wintz An Efficient Three-Dimensional Aircraft Recognition Algorithm Using Normalized Fourier Descriptors *Computer Graphics and Image Processing*, 13, 99-126, 1980.

[97] Emo Welzl Smallest Enclosing Disks (Balls and Ellipsoids) *"New Results and new Trends in Computer Science", Lecture Notes in Computer Science*,555(359-370), 1991.

[98] D. White, and R. Jain Similarity Indexing with the $SS - Tree$. *Proceedings of the 12th International Conference on Data Engineering (ICDE)*, 1996.

[99] K. Wu, A.D. Narasimhalu, B.M. Mehtre, C.P. Lam, and Y.J. Gao CORE: A content-based retrieval engine for multimedia information systems. *Multimedia Systems*, no. 3, p. 25-41, 1995.

[100] C. Yang, and T. Lozano-Perez   Image Database Retrieval with Multiple-Instance Learning Techniques *In the Proceedings of the 16th International Conference on Data Engineering (ICDE)*, San Diego, CA, USA, February 29 - March 3, 2000.

[101] Zhisheng You, and Anil K. Jain Performance Evaluation of Shape Matching via Chord Length Distribution *Proceedings of Computer Vision, Graphics, and Image Processing*, Vol. 28, pp. 129-142, 1984.

[102] K. Zimmermann, and C. Freksa   Qualitative Spatial Reasoning Using Orientation, Distance, and Path Knowledge *IJCAI Workshop on Spatial and Temporal Reasoning, Chambery*, August 1993.

Topic Index